M000116749

# Cougars, Poptarts & One Night Stands

## 101 Essential Wingman Tips

BILLY CONROY

Copyright © 2008 Billy Conroy
All rights reserved.

ISBN: 1-4196-9826-5
ISBN-13: 9781419698262

Visit www.booksurge.com to order additional copies.

# TABLE OF CONTENTS

# V) Special Situations 175

# INTRODUCTION

This book is about getting laid. Sorry to put it so bluntly, but that's just how it is. I have partied with a lot of fun people, developed a lot of friendships, been all over the world on a shoe string, and slept with more women than I can remember. I have tried every approach to meeting women. I know what works and what doesn't work. What I bring to the table regarding knowledge on how to get laid, you will find, is unsurpassed. With all of my experiences I have learned a great deal. I have acquired knowledge that would take decades to learn on your own. I have had more than my share of crazy and humorous experiences. I intend to share all of that knowledge and some of those experiences.

Who am I? Let me tell you who I am not. I am not a male model. I don't have a ten inch schlong. I don't know any celebrities. I'm not rich and I'm not famous. I just love to chase women. I like everything about women and I enjoy the pursuit more than anything. Sleeping with a woman for the first time is one the greatest experiences a man can have.

I love different types of women. Variety is a huge turn-on. Banging more than one girl a week is exciting. I enjoy dating multiple women at one time. I enjoy banging multiple women at one time. I like meeting women. I like being social. Basically, I like women. A true love has developed for 'the chase.' That has made me a connoisseur and an authority on the subject, and, as you will see, a fun guy to party with.

During recent years, I have brushed aside all of the things I realize do not work when trying to meet women. I have focused solely on what works. The results have been extraordinary. I got laid a fair amount when I was younger, but I struck out a lot too. Now I strikeout less, but get laid just as often, if not more. I've been laid more times than anybody I know, but I am still shocked and thrilled when I wake up next to a chick I barely know and the room smells like sex. I love that! I always expect to hook up when I go out, but I am still amazed when I meet a chick and get a blowjob from her a few hours later. The following day I try to analyze what I did right to get the girl home with me, what I did right to close the deal, or what I did wrong to let her get away. Repetition is the best form of education. After a while I came to realize what works and that's what these wingman tips are all about.

Here is one thing that you won't find in this book. I won't be telling you what to say. If that is what you are looking for, please let me know when you find it. If there were certain words I could say to a girl that would assure me of getting laid, that would be more valuable than gold. I certainly wouldn't be sharing them in this book! (I'd be too busy traveling from sorority to sorority.)

Here is another thing you won't find in this book. If you are a dude who is, say a 4 on the scale of 1 - 10, and you expect to read this book and start hooking up with 9s and 10s, let me tell ya brutha, it ain't gonna happen. Others might promise you that, but I can't turn water into wine. Instead, you'll start banging more 5s and 6s, maybe some 7s. For example, I consider myself a 7. I carry myself like a 9. I bang tons of 7s and 8s. I also tap some 9s and 10s, sometimes a 4 or a 5. The point is to be realistic.

You're not going to find any relationship advice in this book either. If that is what you want, go read some other book, or get out of your current relationship and start banging hot chicks. I don't pretend to have all the answers. I just get laid a lot. If you had the opportunity to have a master ladies man as your wingman, you would surely do better with women right? This book will be your wingman.

Another thing you won't find in this book is how to be nice and meet that special lady you want to marry. There are no lessons here on how to be nice. Every knob out there knows how to be nice and get laid once a year. We intend to push the envelope and score much more frequently.

Lastly, there won't be any run of the mill getting-laid-after-the-third-date stories in this book. My friends and I have hundreds of stories of meeting women, taking them out a on a date, then taking them out again on a 2nd date, then calling them over to watch a movie, and then having sex. Boring! (Not boring to do, boring to read) None of those standard getting laid stories will be in this book. Those happen often and are a normal forte. No need for those here. What will be in this book are the out of the ordinary things that have happened. And yes, everything in this book is 100% true.

# I. The Chase

# 1. No Phone Numbers

Is that what you want? If a phone number is what you want, follow these instructions: Fold this book closed right now while keeping your left index finger on this page, hold the book tight with both hands and firmly smack yourself in the forehead with this book. Then open it back up and continue reading.

A phone number is not going to get your rocks off. Getting laid is what you really want! We are not phone number guys. Our goal when my friends and I go out is never to get a girl's phone number. When we go out, we are the guys intending to get laid *that night.* Or at least a blowjob. That should be your goal as well. Yes, we are different than most guys. Most guys are too timid or too inexperienced to attempt to score *that night.*

Granted, we go out a majority of the time and we do not score that night. But many times we do! And that is the ultimate goal.

Often times when we are trying to score with a chick, she only gives up her phone number; that is fine too. Phone numbers are always good, but they are never the primary goal. Here is how it works. The guy who goes out with the intention of taking a girl home that night either succeeds, or he gets a phone number. The guy going out with the intention of getting a girl's phone number, well he just gets to chat with some girl, and she doesn't give out her digits most of the time. And the guy that is just hoping to *talk* to a girl, well he doesn't get jack shit. Do you see where we are going with this? Go out with high expectations. Go out with the idea of trying to score that night. You will end up giving off a vibe of a confident and fun guy, and that is what chicks want. That will lead to you either getting laid that night, or using that phone number to get laid in the near future.

## 2. Watch For Girls Doing Shots

Imagine you're in a bar right now. Some chick comes over to you and says, "Hey! I'm in an unusually wild and frisky mood tonight; I'm very glad to be out. I want to party! Who knows where the night will take me." What would you think? Your boner would pop out of your pants! You'd definitely want to pursue that girl.

Well that is exactly what girls doing shots are saying!

I can't believe more guys don't pay attention to this. More pussy for me! You should always keep your eyes peeled for girls doing shots. This may seem obvious, but I rarely see guys take advantage of this. This is a *clear cut* sign that girls want to party! If they just wanted to hang out and be mellow, they would have a cocktail or a glass of wine. The only reason they are doing shots of alcohol is because it is a special night. They want to get drunk and wild as soon as possible.

I recommend going in to talk to these chicks within 5 to 10 minutes after you see them do a shot. If you wait too long they might get too drunk or some other vultures in the bar might get to them first.

These girls will definitely be open to being approached. You can break the ice and chat with them and lay the foundation. Then the alcohol will hit them. They'll start to like you. They might want to go dance. They might want to do another shot. They might want to start making out. They might want to go to your place and get naked.

If I see girls doing shots, I will watch them and look for the right opportunity to jump in there and say something. A line I might throw out is, "Is tonight a special occasion?" Then, depending on how they respond to that, I follow up with another question based on their answer to my first question.

Girls don't go out to bars and do shots every time they go out. In fact, they rarely do. When girls are doing shots you can narrow down the reasons why quite easily. Maybe it is one of the girl's birthdays. Maybe one of the girls is in town visiting others. Maybe they are all on vacation. Maybe one girl got dumped by her man and she needs to drown her sorrows. Maybe they are just horny cougars, or slutty poptarts. All, and I mean all, of these reasons result in one thing - these girls want cock. They want to hook up sooner or later *that night*. Make no mistake about it.

Have you ever seen a girl do a shot and then say "Ok, now I am going to go home and watch Sex In The City?" No way. Girls doing shots are definitely primary targets. Take this advice and run with it.

## 2. Watch For Girls Looking Around

Most girls at a bar or nightclub are hanging out with their friends or dancing or drinking. They are waiting to be hit on by men. There are some, however, who really want to party. They are too impatient to wait, so they are going to look around the bar and attempt to make some eye-contact in order to expedite the hooking-up process. Watch for girls looking around.

Every so often you will be out at a club and you will see a horny girl and her friend having fun but also looking around. Yeah sure, girls who do this are never the super hot ones, but they *are* the ones who are ready to party *that night.* This trait is often found in cougars, lushes, girls with new boobs, and chicks who are newly single, among others. Women looking around can only be doing it for one of two reasons. They are either waiting for their boyfriend to show up, or they are looking for cock.

You need to assess the situation and figure out which one it is. This isn't hard to do. If they are looking at the front door or the bathroom, and they don't have that Fuck-me-now look, they are probably looking for their dude. If they are looking around the bar or the dance floor, sipping their cocktails from their straw in a sexy seductive manner, checking out other dudes, that means they are looking for cock. Occasionally you will see chicks on the dance floor looking around almost begging for a guy to step up and hit on them. Do it! This is a golden opportunity. For this scam it is best to establish eye contact first, then go in. Nine times out of ten they will be very receptive.

My buddy Carter, his cousin Roger, & myself were at Nero's nightclub in Lake Tahoe when we took full advantage of this. It was early, only a few people there. We were drinking, watching for any hotties that might be rolling in. There were only a handful of people on the dance floor. As we were studying the chicks on the dance floor, we noticed one of them was a smoking hot blond, and her friend, an 8 and 6.5, respectively. The blond was a little older, borderline cougar. She was wearing a black blouse and skirt - you could tell right away she was ready to party. It wasn't hard to recognize. She was looking around every so often, giggling with her friend, etc.

Roger and I say fuckit, let's go in. We went up on the dance floor (we were pretty sober) and just started dancing near them. I made a little eye contact. Then I made some comment about the song that was playing. Some lame Backstreet

Boys song was playing and I said to her, "This is my favorite song." She smiled; she knew I was being sarcastic. That's all it took! It was on like Donkey Kong. Roger was in with her friend too. Nice!

They were in Tahoe on a weekend getaway. My chick had just got dumped by her boyfriend. This was setting up nicely.

We ended up going to the bar for more drinks. The club was filling up and we were having a pretty good time. We went to the corner of the lounge area. The four of us sat down on this padded bench against the wall facing the dance floor. No table in front of us, just the bench we were sitting on. My girl was into me right way. She was on vacation, newly single, and very horny. Can you blame her?

After fifteen or twenty minutes of drinking, talking, flirting and a little kissing, I took her hand and put it on my crotch to see what would happen.

She liked it and started rubbing it. That made me happy. I was pretty drunk too, so I figure, what the hell, I will take it out and maybe she will grab it and stroke me for a while. That would be cool. We were in the corner and I figured who cares if somebody sees; we won't be back in this town for a long time. Plus it was pretty dark in there. I unbuttoned three buttons and whipped it out. She looked at it, leaned in close as if she was about to kiss me, and then, to my astonishment, she went straight down on my schlong like a rat does cheese. I was shocked! And thrilled! What a good girl. She just started suckin dick right off the bat, no questions asked.

In my stupor I look over to my left to see if Roger is noticing this. His girl had her back to us. He kinda looked over her shoulder to see why I was looking at him. His eyes almost popped out of his head. We had only met these girls 45 minutes ago. He attempted to quickly recover his facial expression and act like nothing was happening, but it was too late. His girl turned her head to see what was going on, and I remember her reaction. She said in a normal tone, "Oh no, is she getting sick again?" Apparently, she thought her friend was leaning over getting ready to be sick. Wrong. She's leaning over gagging on my cock. Then Rog's girl saw my girl's head continuously going up and down. She figured out what was going on. She gasped and quickly turned back around towards Roger, muttering "Ohhhh." Roger gave me a smile like, "Dude, you are my hero," and then hugged his chick and tried to make her relax.

Mean time, I began to realize, it's not only very cool that she is giving me a blowjob here in the middle of the club, but, she is giving me *one hell* of a super blowjob. I still remember it to this day. It was a Top 5 Blowjob of all time. She was really going to town down there, and doing some incredible vacuum thing with her mouth. Jacking the shaft perfectly; man, this chick could really suck dick. I couldn't see anything except for the back of her bleach blond hair, but boy did it feel incredible. Then I began to realize Mt St Helens was about to erupt. There was nothing I could do, so I just let it go.

Good girl did her best to cap the well, but it went everywhere. I lost control. I had my head tilted back against the nightclub wall, looking up. I let out a deep, drawn out moan. It was like a triple orgasm or something. Fricken incredible.

After what seemed like a long time, I gathered myself and realized I needed to clean up a little. Thankfully, nobody in the club was sitting there staring. I don't know how they could have missed it, but they did.

I needed to get some napkins. I could either zip up, making things more messy, and go all the way over to the mens room (which was outside of the club), or I could not zip up and head around the corner to the bar and get some napkins. I went to the back bar, with my cock still out. The back bar was not busy, only a few people there. Who was hanging out in the corner of the bar, randomly? Yup, my main man Carter! He immediately said, "Dude, where have you been? There are some chicks here! I can't find Roger either." I reached for napkins and said, "Dude, I just got a blowjob in the corner over there; I need to clean up a little." I started cleaning my johnson off right there. Carter looked down and could see I was telling the truth from the mess all over my pants and the fact that my Johnson was out and I was cleaning it. He was speechless.

I went back to where my girl was and hung out for a while. She thought I was going to leave because I got what I wanted. Normally I would, but I decided to hang out with her regardless. That made her happy. She was actually a cool chick whose wealthy greystoke boyfriend treated her like shit. She told me all about it. We hung out for another hour. Roger took his girl out to their Chevy Suburban and got a blowjob. I took my girl out to Carter's work truck and bent her over the front seat while I stood outside and drilled her nice & good.

It was an all around epic night. Carter didn't hook up but he was glad that his cousin and I did. And it was all because we recognized these two chicks looking around.

## 4. The Best Opening Line

The best opening line in the world is......drum roll please......*not* something you have planned, rehearsed, or memorized. It is something that just comes to you as you approach the girl! I know, many will say this is no help. I highly recommend going in with a question. No formal introduction, just a question. Don't make it, "Where are you from?" That is overused and does not inspire a girl to talk to you. (Only ask her that after you have spoken with her for a while.) Force yourself to approach an attractive woman and I guarantee something will come out of your mouth. Ask her a question. Ask her opinion. Ask her something. I have even witnessed a buddy go in and talk to a girl who most would think was way out of his league with this line "Hi." She turned to look him, and he said,

"I don't have anything like an opening line; I just wanted to talk to you." I saw her smile slightly and look him in the eyes and I knew he was in. Then he said something like "Are you having a good time?" and she just started rambling on. He just nodded a couple times and the conversation was on.

Find something about her that you can ask her a question about; her appearance, her clothes, her hair, her opinion, etc. Find something about your surroundings to talk about. There are many questions you can ask. Remember the best line is not a line, it something that you just came up with. Women respect that more than anything. The best opening line in the world is a random question.

# 5. Good Opening Lines

If I can't find something unique to say I still have some fall back lines that might pop out if the timing is right, or if I'm too drunk to think of something witty. These usually are good ice-breakers:

"How's your night going?"

"You look like you are in a good mood."

"What is that you are drinking?"

"Cheers!" (just put your drink and say cheers and look for a response.)

"You look like you could use a drink."

"I like your earrings."

"Is tonight a special occasion; why are there so many of you girls out?" (used for a large group of girls).

"Good music here huh, I like this DJ."

"How come you're not out there dancing?"

"Wanna do a shot?"
"I like your hair. It looks great."

Here's a quick example of me being cocky and opening it up with a hot chick. I was at this bar sitting with my buddy drinking a pint of beer. The table next to us had this really attractive older chick, blond, short hair, dark tan, probably 30 or 31. She was definitely the hottest chick in the bar. She was with some total dork. He had a mustache, a red Hawaiian shirt, and was in his late 30s. My buddy and I couldn't believe she was rolling with guy. This knob finally went to the bathroom and I casually said to her, "You have pretty earrings."

She turned to see if I was talking to her, and saw me looking directly at her. She said, "Oh thank you."

I paused briefly, then said, "You havin a good time?"

"Oh yes. We came up from Miami just for the weekend. We are having a great time."

I said "Oh Miami, that's cool. You and your brother came up for the weekend?"

She looked at me, paused for a second, and then said, "He's my boyfriend, not my brother." I paused, and then said "Oh." Hopefully I made her feel a little awkward for being with that shmuck. He came back from the bathroom and all four us talked for a little while about Chicago. She let on that she was an interior designer and I told her I was looking for a good one. Later, when they left, she came up to me and handed me her business card. Her boyfriend couldn't see the look she gave me, but she basically gave me the look of 'call me sometime so we can flirt, fondle, & fuck.' They left. My buddy Johnny said that was *money* how I worked that chick. Two weeks later I was in Miami for business. I sent her a text message on Saturday afternoon. She met me out that evening. By midnight we were naked in my hotel room. All because of "You have pretty earrings."

Keep in mind all of these are just openers and the next thing you say after the opener is very important. You have to be ready to fire right back quickly depending on her response to the first question. This is key. The second thing you say to her after you get a response from her is just as important as your opening line. So sharpen your wit and be ready to respond to her reply.

## 6. Don't Use the Same Line Dummy

My buddy Party Scars (more on him later) thought he had a great line. It was, "I have been waiting all night to talk to you." It was kind of funny because he would bump into a girl, turn around, and say that line. It was working pretty well, but he completely over-used it. I remember us leaving the club at closing and Party Scars saying that line to a girl who was with two of her girlfriends. She got a big smile on her face and seemed thrilled that Scars was so interested in her. But then her other friend loudly blurted out, "You said that *same* line to me over by the bar!" Then all three girls gave Scars a dirty look, scurried away, and Scars felt like a jackass. So mix up your openers. And remember the best opener of all is not something you have thought of ahead of time.

## 7. Where to Stand in a Bar

Let's say you are in a bar. It's packed. Groups of girls, poptarts, cougars, all types of chicks everywhere. Now let's say you are sitting *under* the table. What are your mathematical chances of meeting a girl sitting under the table? I will answer for you. They are 1%. 99% chance you won't score.

Now, let's be realistic. What if I told you that standing by the entrance inside the bar you have a 15% chance of meeting a chick, but if you stand over by the ladies restroom, you have a 27% chance of meeting a girl? Where would you stand?

It's very important where you choose to hang out in a bar or nightclub. One of the worst places to stand is near the entrance. When chicks walk in, they want to get in and have a look around, not get hit on as soon as they step in the place. Standing on the edge of the dance floor is another bad idea. I see this all too often: Guys will be congregating near the dance floor, staring at chicks dancing, hoping to meet chicks entering the dance floor or coming off the dance floor. Some guys think that if they stare at a girl, she will stare back and invite him to come dancing. Doesn't work that way pal.

You need to stand in a good place, be the man, and step up and approach a woman. A good place to stand is by the bar. This is a high traffic area and interaction is very easy. You'll almost always find me by the bar. I even prefer to stand near the bar rather than getting a table and bottle service! The bar is where all the action is. The ladies room is another smart place to position your crew. Every chick in the place will be hitting the toilet sooner or later. You can pick them off on the way back out. Hanging out by the DJ can also be good, but I prefer the bar and near the ladies bathroom. So, when you enter the venue, make it a point to find the best place to hang out and your probability of meeting chicks will increase.

# 8. Ordering Drinks at the Bar

Ordering drinks at the bar is the ideal time to meet women. It's easy to nonchalantly make a comment to a girl or ask her a question while waiting to order drinks. Women feel less threatened with this approach. They believe your primary objective is to get a cocktail. Little do they know ~ your primary objective is always to meet chicks.

Sure, half the time you make a comment and the girl just moves on, but half the time it can turn into a starter conversation. When I spot a hot chick near the bar I meander over there. I get in line to order drinks. I just want to be near her, in her proximity, and prepared to open up some kind of small talk. I might not even need a drink! I have thrown away $12 dollar Kettle One & Red Bulls just to go order a new drink near a hot chick. While other jackasses are fighting for the bartender's attention I'll be waiting patiently, working the hot chick in line.

Taking your time when ordering is a wise decision. If the bartender doesn't see you, that's fine. This gives you more time to hang out there in the close proximity of eligible women. Any situation can arise. Say some girl is ordering drinks or shots for her girlfriends I might say, "What's the special occasion?" Or say she is drinking a foo-foo drink (daiquiri, pina colada, etc) I might act a little surprised and say, "What is *that* you are drinking?" If she looks sophisticated and horny I might offer to buy her a shot. If nothing comes to mind I can always fall back on "I like your hair," or any crap like that.

Be aware of your body language. Always appear to be facing the bar, or slightly facing the bar. Facing your target looks like you are coming on too strong. She might not like that. Your body language should make her understand that you are just being friendly and not hitting on her. You're just making small talk while waiting to order drinks. This is how many good encounters begin. Once she is receptive or you can tell she is interested in talking, then you can face her and proceed with building rapport.

## 9. Women Read Body Language

Women read your body language. Be aware of your body language. Improve the signal you are giving off. Have good posture. Keep your shoulders back. Don't sit there with your arms folded. Don't have both hands in your pockets like you just lost your puppy. Don't sulk or show that you are in a bad mood. If you are in a bad mood, go home. Act happy. Have a playful smirk on your face like you are thinking of a dirty joke.

Ever wonder why once you get a girlfriend, chicks start hitting on you or flirting with you *all the time*?! It is because you have a subtle happy smirk on your face (because you're getting laid on a regular basis). This is good body language. Chicks pick up on this vibe, and that is the type of person they want to be with. If you want to give off a good vibe, act like you just got laid or you just won the lottery. It will do wonders for your game.

## 10. Break The Seal

Ever arrive at a bar or party, then wait until you have a drink or two before considering to talk to the opposite sex? Then an hour goes by and you feel like shmuck for not being more outgoing. Then the night slips away and you wasted a good opportunity?

When you arrive at a bar, nightclub, party, or any event, step up to the plate and talk to any chick in your proximity, asap! It might be your waitress, the bartender, the ugly chick next to you, a fat chick at the buffet, a horny milf, some guy's girlfriend, the hot chick walking by, anybody. This will break the seal and you will end up talking to chicks all night. If you wait too long to break the seal, you might get in a funk and have no desire to step up and break the ice with any women. Once you have broken the seal, you will simply be more comfortable talking to women.

I have seen guys go the whole night without talking to one woman! This will not be tolerated. Talk to just one girl, early on, every night. This is a start. Once you have talked to one, you can talk to ten. Other chicks notice when guys are talking to other chicks, or making other chicks laugh. Subconsciously, women are attracted to this. So it is always a good idea to begin talking to chicks around you, no matter where you are. It is a fact; women are more attracted to men talking with other women. Break the seal!

An example of breaking the seal happened in San Diego a while back. That night we went to this new nightclub in downtown San Diego. It was the new hot spot in town. Because it was such a pain in the ass to get in we got there very early. Scars, Grady, I were hanging out in the side room waiting for other buddies to show up. This room was a dark lounge with a few black leather couches and a bar. There were only a handful of people in this room besides the bartender - a couple dudes smoking cigars, a group in the corner, and three chicks on a bachelorette party. The three of us were sitting there drinking Amstels and shooting the shit. The DJ was playing this cool hip hop mix. Naturally, we start talking to the chicks in our proximity. They didn't look like fun girls, but we wanted to break the seal. Two of them were quiet, but the bachelorette was a little drunk already so she was in a flirty, outgoing mood.

She was very hot, half Asian and half white; a goody-two-shoes looking chick who you could tell doesn't party very often. She had the white bachelorette veil on her head and a small bag of bachelorette toys, condoms and crap like that. These chicks were waiting for the rest of their party to show up.

So the bachelorette pulls out one of her toys from the party. It was a little wind-up penis. It was about 2 inches tall, beige, and it had little feet and would walk if you wound it up. She wound it up and put it on the coffee table. It waddled across the table. We all chuckled and thought it was mildly amusing. Scars being Scars grabs the toy and puts it on his crotch to get a laugh. He smiles like it is his own 2-inch penis.

To our surprise, the bachelorette girl gets up and walks over to Scars. This hot little innocent Asian girl bends over and goes down on the toy for a few seconds! With her mouth, while Scars was holding it near his crotch!

We were like, "Whoa! Alright!" We were laughing. Her friends were laughing, and it was cool. It definitely livened things up a little.

Scars put the toy back on the table. I leaned over from the other chair and grabbed the toy. One thing my friends know about me, I have been known to whip my schlong out at random times. I like to shock people, and I like to make them laugh.

That night I was wearing a dress shirt, un-tucked. My dress shirt was hanging low, so I took the toy penis and put it under my shirt for a second. Everyone would be expecting to see the toy on my crotch, so I thought it would be funny to pulled out my real penis instead. I unzipped my zipper and pulled my soft pig out and lifted up my shirt. I was holding my real penis there, for the whole world to see. Scars and Grady had seen me do this before, so they were laughing but not that hard. The other chicks across on the other couch were laughing too.

The bachelorette got up and started coming over to me. I had no idea why. She gets close to me. She scoots down low and starts to bend over. My best guess was she is going to pretend to suck it so she can get a laugh. I've pulled my hog out many times before and never got a reaction like this. She put her hands on my knees and went down low and completely goes down on me. On my penis! Mouthed my entire soft pig.

We would find out later that this girl always wears glasses, but this was a special night so she left them at home. No contact lenses, no glasses. She thought it was the toy.

So she is down there for few seconds and I can feel her mouth probing around and I can see that she is figuring out that this soft thing in her mouth isn't a hard plastic toy. This thing in her mouth is my cock! Suddenly, she explodes up and jumps on me and starts strangling me. She was pissed! And she was freaking out! I was trying to laugh but I was also trying to peel her hands off my throat. Grady was the closest to me. He was trying to get her off of me, but he was laughing so hard that he had no strength. I will never forget turning to look at Scars for help. He was bright, bright red and there was a tear coming down his face. He was laughing so hard he couldn't even make a noise. He finally came over to help and so did her friend. Her friends got her off me and explained to me that she didn't have her glasses on.

Those chicks didn't hang around much longer. But boy did we have a good night that night. All three us hooked up and brought chicks home. It must have been because we were in a good mood.

## 11. Never Introduce Yourself

When meeting a girl for the first time, skip the introductions. Nice guys introduce themselves. Interesting, confident guys goes straight into conversation. If she wants to know your name, she will ask for it, or she will introduce herself.

An introduction is a waste of time, and it gives off the wrong vibe. Instead, just ask her a question. Or make a comment. If she smiles or acknowledges your comment, then ask her a question. A question is *much* better than an introduction. This is how a conversation begins. And since you didn't formally introduce yourself, she will perceive this discussion as just two people talking, instead of one guy hitting on one girl. A woman can appreciate a discussion. She might let her guard down and talk to you. It's quite possible you may seem interesting to her, or witty, or cute. Whereas, if you formally introduced yourself, the first thing she will think is, "Do I even want to bother talking to this guy?" By skipping the introduction, you are preventing her from considering that notion. She is already caught up in answering your question or having an opinion on your comment.

Now maybe she still blows you off. Well at least you didn't waste extra time by introducing yourself to some lame chick!

After you have talked with her for a while and built some rapport, then you could say, "by the way, my name is...." But please, no immediate introductions.

## 12. Swing The Bat

Get up off the wall and go talk to a chick or two. Swing the bat! Quiet, self-absorbed guys never get the girl. Every successful man to ever walk this earth has taken many chances. Hitting on a chick could result in you getting turned down. So what! It could result in you scoring with a super hot babe who will have you feeling like a champion. That is a trade with great upside potential and very little downside. Those are the risks you want to take. Those who take risks are the only ones who reap the rewards. You will talk to girls who don't give you the time of day. I do. Happens all the time. But some chicks *will* talk to you! And the more times you swing the bat, the better you will become. If you talk to ten chicks in one week, three will be receptive. But with every chick, you gain more experience and more knowledge. Pretty soon four out of ten will be receptive, and so on. Swing the bat, you've got nothing to lose.

## 13.  One's Hot, One's Not

This problem comes up very often. You spot a fine-ass sexy broad across the way. You get excited. You ponder your next move. Then you spot her butt-ugly friend right next to her. What do you do? How do you handle this situation? This is a tough scenario. Many guys go down in flames handling this the wrong way because the ugly chick will cockblock you in a heartbeat if you make the slightest error.

Popular opinion is to go up to both of them and talk to the ugly one to show that you are a cool guy, and then eventually hit on the hot one. I disagree with this tactic. I think phone-number guys like that move. My goal is to get laid, not get a phone number. I have tried that move numerous times, and more times than not, the fricken ugly one lays claim to you. Then you are off limits to the hot one. You look like a jerk when you dog the ugly one and go for the hot one.

One way to handle this predicament is to have your buddy jump on the grenade. This is a good idea on paper, and I have some stellar wingman at my disposal, but very few of them will jump on a fugly chick just to help a brutha out. And rightly so. A guy has to deal with this one on his own.

The best way to handle this situation is to man-up and go directly in and throw your best game at the hot one. The only adjustment you need to make is to involve both of them in the conversation. The best way to do this is to make frequent eye-contact with the ugly one while you are telling your story to the hot one. Talk to both of them. Don't ignore the ugly one! I look at the hot one 70% of the time, and the ugly one 30% of the time. This way the ugly one feels a part of the team and she won't pull her girlfriend away and cockblock you.

Often times you'll find the hot one dragged the ugly one out with her because she was in the mood to party. The hot one expects to get hit on. Hot chicks do not wingman ugly chicks. If the hot chick did not want be hit on, she would have stayed home. So step up and hit on her.

To sum up, there is no ground-breaking wisdom here; if one's hot and one's not, just go headstrong in for the hot one, but keep the ugly one somewhat involved.

## 14. Her Hair

Have you ever seen a girl get ready? How long does it take a chick to get ready for a night out on the town? A long damn time! She spends an incredible amount of time on her hair, making it look just right. She might wash it, blow dry it, curl it, cut it, color it, mousse it, spray it, all kinds of crap. Obviously, they really care about how their hair looks. And do us guys ever notice? Hell no. We look at how their face looks and then immediately at their tits. (And then I always check out their ass, but this is more difficult. Sometimes when I'm in a bar or nightclub I will squat down real low just to get the correct view of a chick's ass. It embarrasses my friends, but I would rather squat down low and have a clear look at her ass, rather than find out she has a large, rotund ass after I am home with her. Hot chicks with large asses are very clever about covering them up. I have hooked up with many a girl only to discover, later that night, some big ole cottage cheese dimple ass later that night that I have to stare at while I am pounding her doggiestyle. Ugghh!)

But I digress. Asses were not the subject. The subject is complimenting a girl on her hair, and that is a great way to start a conversation. Seriously, this is one of my best openers! I use it often. Girls love talking about their hairdo. The compliment is 100% bullshit because I surely don't know much about hair. But it works every time! It's great for two reasons. One, it makes them feel good about themselves. They put all this time into their hair and somebody noticed! Two, it sets you apart and shows that you are original, observant, and into something she is into, her hair! This opener can lead to other conversation topics. Then you will be talking to her, and you can show her your personality. Then you are in, and you can get her back to your place so you can tap that cottage cheese ass.

## 15. The Two Subjects To Never Bring Up

If you like beating-off more than getting laid, talk to girls about their ex-boyfriends. Nothing good can come from the ex-boyfriend conversation. You'll probably put her in a bad mood. Or a sad mood. She might even start to miss him. If this happens, her pussy will shrivel up like a prune and there is no way you are getting laid. She might start going on and on about her ex, and then you'll be classified as one of her 'guy friends' that she confides in. Stay away from the ex conversation.

Also, there is absolutely no upside in asking a girl how old she is, so never do it. All women become self-conscious about their age. Asking their age will likely make them uncomfortable. She might justify her age by telling you she's a MILF and has kids at home and now she doesn't want to party. She might be too young to be in the bar and you will scare her away. She might ask for your age back, and then count you out because you are too young or too old. There are all kinds of reasons, just trust me; there is no need to ever bring up the subject of age.

These rules are set in stone. If you ever see one of your buddies talking about these banned subjects, it is your duty as a bro to pull him aside and set him straight. Let him know both of the banned subjects so he will relate them to each other and then he will understand. One time I saw this dumbass guy get involved in an ex-boyfriend conversation with a chick and her group of girls. He asked her how old she was in front of the whole group. Not only did she get turned off for the night, so did all of her hot slutty friends! I didn't even know this guy, but I went up to him and told him to knock that shit off. He would have gone on cockblocking forever if I wouldn't have set him straight.

## 16. Three Traits All Gigolos Possess

Why is it some guys get laid all the time while others don't? I worked on this problem for years. I observed and analyzed every guy I saw or knew who was getting ass all the time. I was pretty good myself, but watching and emulating these guys made me much better. There are basically three traits that every one of these guys had in common. Here is what they *did not* have in common. Some were rich, some were poor, some were handsome, some were not, some were short, some were tall, some were educated, some were uneducated, some were young, and some were older.

The three things all gigolos, or guys who get laid a lot, have in common are:

a) They were all **confident** guys. Women are attracted to confident men. It is a fact. And the more confident the better. I have seen the hottest chicks with guys whose only thing going for them is that they are cocky. The dude might be broke, have a funny looking face, or be in terrible shape, but he has hot-ass chick under his arm. In fact, take a look at all the smoking hot chick's boyfriends you see for the next couple weeks. You will see that every one of them is with a confident or cocky guy.

Let me tell you, confidence is *not* a quality you are born with. You can earn it, you can develop it, and you can even fake it. When I was in high school I had zero self-confidence. And of course I never got laid. To change this, I observed others around me, watched a few Clint Eastwood movies, got laid a couple times, and developed my own brand of confidence. At first, I realized I needed to fake this confidence thing so I can meet more women and get laid. So I did. And it worked! Then, gradually, I realized that I didn't need to fake it anymore because there was no reason for me *not* to be confident. It eventually turned into legitimate confidence and I became very good at meeting women.

So be confident, shit, be cocky! And you will see positive results. Keep in mind that by simply approaching a woman, you are exuding confidence.

b) Guys who get laid a lot are all **jovial**. Be happy. Be a fun guy. If you are jovial or laughing a lot, women want to be in your sphere of influence. Women can read your vibe much better than you think. If you are fun, women want to be around you. Give off a positive vibe and you are guaranteed to have women attracted to you.

c) The third trait that all guys who hook up with lot of woman have is that they deal with being shot down very well. They have developed a **thick skin**. These guys don't give two shits if they are denied by a chick. Every time I get shot down I say to myself, 'Well at least I tried.' I have heard my buddy Mike tell friends, "I love being shot down." He rationalizes it because he says it is the second best thing to hooking up. The third being the guys who stands by the wall all night afraid to talk to a chick. And the fourth being the guy who stays home and doesn't even give himself a shot. Listen, women will never approach you. Don't dream of that happening. That teenage after-school movie where the girl smiles at the guy and then makes the first move is not real life. Get that thought out of your head. The only guys who get anywhere in this world are guys who go out there and take chances. Bruce Lee said "There is no help but self help." You need to go out and approach women and get shot down and that's how it works. Once it doesn't bother you, woman will come to you easily.

One night in Palo Alto I saw my buddy Giles get shot down eight consecutive times! That would rattle most men, but not Giles. He was confident and jovial and walking up to groups of chicks. He was throwing his arm over their shoulders and saying stuff like, "Who's in a good mood here?!" I have seen this dude bag some of the hottest women ever, so I know he has game, even though I was watching him get shot down left and right. I tried talking to a couple chicks and wasn't faring much better, so it was looking like it might be a tough night. Then I saw Giles do his patented move, the hand grab, to this cute redhead. (Giles grabs a girl firmly by the hand, pulls her in a little bit, and then says something happy to them. It's a money move I must say.)

So I don't see him for a long time after. I thought my bro might have left or went to get food. It was not like him to leave his wingman. Finally I found him by the bar a couple hours later. The club was going off now; I had some chicks with me so I was partying. I said to him "Bro, where they heck were you?" He starts to tell me. While he's talking to me I look at his pants and he has two bright green grass stains on his faded Diesel jeans. He also has grass stains on his elbows, his fly is halfway undone, his hair is all messed up, and there is big grass-dirt clump sticking out of his dress shoe.

I start laughing as he starts telling me his story. Apparently, he and this redhead, Anna, went up to the Los Altos foothills about 15 minutes away. They took a walk, trespassing on someone's property. It was a tall grass field that was barb-wired off. They wanted to lie in the grass and look at the stars. (great line Giles!) He said he laid her down and they started hooking up and I remember him telling me he went straight for her 'wiskerbiscuit.' He went down on her, then they started having sex. He said it was great because it was a hot summer night and they were drunk and running on those basic instincts when you just first meet someone. Then he said he was 'hitting it' and they were on an incline and gravity was pulling her into him and he was really killin' that 'pootananny.' He didn't care about anything accept hitting it.

Afterwards, he was really worried I would leave, so he rushed back. So that's how he got the grass stains and the dirt all over himself. Dirty sex in a wet grass field out in the hills. Love it. I don't tell the story as good as he told me in person that night, but his feeling was one of euphoria, pure summertime delight, and I'll never forget how happy he was telling me that story. Most guys would have thrown in the towel, but not Giles.

I made him hang out with me for the final two hours until the club closed. Every five minutes I would look over at his filthy clothes a laugh my ass off. I had a hot poptart with me; I met her while Giles was gone. (Poptart = hot young girl, 18-23, ready to party) I tried to set Giles up with her friend. She was hot too. She wanted nothing to do with Giles because he looked like he had just rolled around in a field.

Giles was really feeling it though. He had just got laid so he was beaming. Somehow he sweet-talked that chick and an hour later they were making out. All four of us hit the dance floor. Dudes were looking at Giles and saying, "What the hell?! Look how dirty that dude is!" We all just laughed.

When the club closed we all went back to my chick's apartment. It was really a great night. All because Giles never gave up.

## 17. Laugh A Lot

Do me a favor. Think about the office you work in and your co-workers, or the people you do business with. Out of all of those people, who laughs the most? What person do you see laughing the most often? Now that you have that person in mind, here is the next question. Do you like that person or dislike that person?

I am pretty sure that your answer will be 'like them.'

Now do the same thing with your family & friends. Who laughs the most? Do you like that person? I bet you do.

The following tip is one you can use throughout life, not just with chicks. Laugh a lot! This might be one of the most important points made in this book. Make a conscious effort to laugh more often in more situations. People love someone who isn't afraid to express themselves with laughter, to laugh out loud, and to laugh out loud *often*. Women are attracted to happy, fun guys. This is a fact! What better way to show you are a happy, fun guy than to laugh a lot. This is one of the few things men can do to separate themselves and show women that they are someone with a zest for life.

If you are observant, you will find many occasions which can elicit laughter. Maybe you are talking to chick you just met and she said something funny. Laugh out loud and don't be shy about it. Maybe you are at a bar and you overhear a girl's comment about another girl. Laugh out loud. The girl will turn to see if you are laughing at her comment. Subconsciously, she will enjoy the compliment of you thinking that her comment was funny. It could lead to you getting to know her.

When my friends and I are hanging out, you'll hear us laughing a lot. At a bar, hanging out getting some food, watching a ballgame, sitting at a blackjack table; it doesn't matter where. We are boisterous, we are fun, and we are not shy about it. This, undoubtedly, causes attention to be drawn to us. Even if I am with one buddy, just the two of us talking to each other and laughing at some story will give off a good vibe. Women want to be around laughter.

## 18. Women Love to Hear Their Own Name

All Women love to hear their own name. In fact, all people do. This is actually a great business skill as well. I have become good friends with people in the business world due to me unexpectedly calling them by their first name. People remember this. You can be darn sure that they will make an effort to find out your name and use it next time. The same goes for meeting chicks. Call them by their first name and they will look at you in a different light. Even better if you are in the middle of a story and you say, "You know what I'm talking about Kim?" She will nod yes and subconsciously she will start paying closer attention. She will also be impressed that you remembered her name.

The Name Tip reminds me of my buddy Brady. Now whatever you do, don't call a girl by the wrong name - unless you are going for a Rodeo Screw. My buddy Brady was having sex with this girl he just met, Samantha, while we were on a road trip in Miami. (It was late night, and a few of us came home empty handed; naturally, we were at the door listening to everything.)

Brady was hammered and apparently in the mood to Rodeo Screw. I've heard other renditions, but to correctly Rodeo Screw someone you have to be in the middle of having sex with a girl, call her by the wrong name, more than once, loudly, and then hold on for at least 8 seconds.

So Brady was doing this girl doggie and he starts belting out, "Oh Karen, you feel so good." (Karen was his ex-girlfriend) Samantha just ignored it. Samantha was a real skanky broad, kind of a cute face, skinny body but not firm, pancake boobs, dark dyed hair, trampstamp tattoo above her ass of some tribal crap, a little butterfly tattoo on the side of her waist, and one other tattoo we would soon discover.

She looked good in the dark nightclub. Strobe light honey though. Brady thought she was hot and took her out of there back to our hotel. Brady was boning her and he continued, "Oh Karen, you know you love it! Oh yeah baby." Samantha finally turned and snarled at him, "My name is Samantha!" hoping that would clear things up. Brady responded drunkenly, "Oh yeah *Karen*, I'm gonna do you aaaaall night long.... You like that cock huhhh Karen!" Samantha began to struggle and we were all grabbing each other and really cracking up at the door, but trying to keep quiet.

Brady held her by the waist, "Karen, stay here baby..." and then she really started squirming around trying to get free. Brady was doing pretty well, and he actually lasted for about

9 or 10 seconds. We could tell she got free because we heard a big "urgghh," and then we heard her feet hit the floor. She came stomping towards us so we scrambled. The bathroom was not in the bedroom, so we realized she was coming out. I was on my knees and couldn't move away fast enough though. She opened the door and came stomping by us and straight into the bathroom. As she walked by I saw her third tattoo, close up. It was right above her pussy. It said "RUDY" in cursive letters. It wasn't a small tattoo either; it was a couple inches tall! Now that's a tattoo.

Brady told us later she was a stripper, and that when he started fooling around with her, he got her naked and noticed the ex-boyfriend Rudy tattoo. He immediately lost any respect he had for her, so a Rodeo Fuck was in order.

That is the only time of have heard of the Rodeo Fuck pulled off successfully.

## 19. Use Nicknames

Once you meet a chick, call her by some variation of her name. The hotter the girl, the more you should rely on some variation of her name. Calling a girl by a nickname will set you apart. This helps break down barriers and makes her feel like she knows you better than she actually does.

I met a model chick Abbey, and started calling her Abs right away that night - I think it showed that I was comfortable with her and not shy. She dogged every guy she talked to but was cool hanging out with me. We exchanged digits and to my surprise, *she* called *me* a couple nights later. When she called, I said, "What's up Abigail?!" Now when I run into her I say, "Abs of steel! What's up girl?!" and she loves it. It's like were old buddies.

I met a chick through another chick and I quickly forgot her name. She had just been on a trip to Miami and looked super tan and hot. I just started calling her 'South Beach.' I ran into her a few nights later and said, "South Beach! What's up girl?!" She loved it. Banged her a few nights later.

I knew a chick Liz, I always called her Elizabeth. Megan, I called her Megs right away and we were like best buds. Sonya, well I called her Sonya-I-wanna-bone-ya, but never to her face. And so on and so forth. Doing subtle things like using nicknames will make chicks remember you.

## 20. The Art Of Touch

Initial conversation with a girl is very important, obviously. There are subtle things you can do to let her know you are attracted to her. There are subtle things you can do to set off her sexual sensors that will result in her unknowingly becoming attracted to you. This is done through laughter, through engaging conversation, and through touch. We will discuss touch.

When I am talking to a girl, I am trying to build rapport. Usually this only takes a few minutes. As soon I sense rapport, I am subconsciously trying to exude sexuality and build attraction. While I am trying to make a point in my conversation, I will casually and nonchalantly touch her on the side of her waist. I will also touch her on the waist if I have just said something funny. I'll be looking away in laughter but at the same time holding her waist, or the small of her back. This little touch on the waist goes a long way. This subtle touch helps to break down the 'stranger' wall and gets you closer to 'friendly' status. It also lets her know you might be attracted to her.

I will also use touch if we are going to move locations. I will touch her gently by the waist or her lower back and guide her for a split second. This is a masculine thing to do, and it is a gentlemen thing to do. This move may come natural to some guys. But many guys see it as forbidden territory to touch a girl. This must be overcome.

Gently and briefly grabbing a girl on her side, above her jeans, on her waist, is a move that lets a woman know you are masculine and confident. The importance of this cannot be understated. This is the first step in letting her know you are different. I can't tell you how many times this has been the first step in getting a chick stimulated and on her way to sleeping with me by the end of the night.

Have you ever been hanging out in a bar, and a woman touches you to so she can walk by? Your first reaction is, 'Damn that felt kind of good. Is some chick hitting on me?' You swing around to see who it was and why she is touching you like that. You discover it's just some girl passing by, trying to get through. This is an example of you being stimulated by touch. Women are the same way. Most guys won't touch a girl because women are unfamiliar to them. I am around women all the time, so I am familiar with them, and touch is not a big deal. Every guy who scores with a lot of girls is a master of the subtle touch.

If you do have conversation with touch involved, there is no doubt she will be stimulated. She will put you in a different category. She will be trying to figure out if you are just a guy who is touchy-feely, or if you are actually interested in her. She'll also start asking herself if she is attracted to you.

What about when you are dancing with a girl? The more touching the better! Even if you are dancing apart, you should be grabbing her by the waist or by the hands every so often.

What about when you find yourself sitting next to girl? If I am sitting next to a girl talking to her, maybe in a bar or nightclub, I will put my hand on her knee or right above her knee very briefly. I do this approximately once every five minutes, and only for a couple seconds. This needs to be done at the right moment. I do it, but only when I am making a point in the conversation, or I am looking away in laughter, or if I am going to get up and move. Notice that in all three situations, we are preoccupied by something else, so the touch is a secondary thing and supposedly unnoticed. That is the subtle way touch leads to attraction.

## 21. Questions When They Like You

Once you have been talking or hanging out with a chick, you need to be able to recognize things a woman says as signs that she is into you. Her body language is also important. Both of these are the keys to identifying attraction. A woman will not tell you how they feel, you have to figure it out. Recognizing a possible attraction will give you a great advantage on how to proceed. Maybe she is turning her back to you or folding her arms and not into you. You should abort. Maybe she hasn't asked you one question about yourself. She is conceded and you should abort. Maybe you want to back off a little because you can tell she likes you a lot, *too* much. Maybe you dig her too and now you can relax that she feels the same way.

One example is when a chick asks, "What is your last name?" I've heard this one a handful of times. Right away, I know I am in. She doesn't realize it, but in the back of her mind she is picturing us together.

More questions women will ask when they are interested in you, and what the woman has in the back of her mind:

"Where do you live?" (if we start dating, hopefully you don't live too far away)

"How old are you?" (I am attracted to you, hopefully you are in my age range)

"I like your jeans, what are those?" (boy do you look sexy in those jeans)

"Do you have brothers or sisters?" (need to know about your family because I can picture myself with you)

"Where did you grow up?" (I just want to know more about you; need to know your background)

"Are you a player?" (you are seducing me and I like it. Hopefully you don't do this all the time)

"Have I seen you before?" (I have to make it obvious that I am interested in you)

"How many women have you slept with?" (Geez, you were so good at seducing me; that worries me)

"Harder! Harder! Will you cum on my face baby?" (I like you so much you can have your way with me)

Most likely you have heard many of these questions at some point in your life. You probably didn't realize that these are all questions asked by a woman very interested in you! These questions are subtle hints that she is attracted to you. Keep an ear out for these questions, and use this knowledge to your advantage.

## 22. A Good Listener

I have a friend who always wants to talk about himself. He'll go on and on about what's happening in *his* life, what *his* day was like, what *his* opinions are, etc. This is a mistake. It's an immediate turnoff with chicks. With the women out there now, you need to be a good listener.

Here is the key to becoming a good listener. Whatever subject she is talking about, ask her a question *directly* related to what she is talking about. A good listener nods occasionally, agreeing with her point. He says, "Oh really" occasionally. He smiles at the appropriate times. He asks inquisitive questions to show he is paying attention. He is empathetic to her point of view. He makes brief eye-contact. He looks away at the appropriate times. Generally, he acts like he understands her. These are the Good Listener methods. Using them will be instrumental in building rapport with chicks.

Looking away is important. Never stare at a chick 100% of the time. You'll look like you are hanging on every word she says. You will be *out* faster than I can say "desperate" if you stare at her 100% of the time. Looking away at the right times is inadvertently showing confidence. At the same time, don't look off into the distance for the entire conversation or you will appear disinterested.

Most guys are not good listeners. Most guys are only thinking of what words they can say next, instead of just focusing on what she is saying. Being a good listener is directly correlated to how much ass you score. Understand that chicks love a good listener! If you do all these things you will be *in*. You will know you are in because she will end up asking you questions about yourself.

# 23. Become A Closer

Countless times I have witnessed a chick being hit on by a guy who can't close. One skill you'll need to master is to be able to spot these situations. It is the same as watching a girl doing shots (mentioned in #2); being able to notice these situations in a bar is extremely important. It separates a phone-number guy from a closer.

When I see a guy fumbling to close a chick I sit back and for some reason I always imagine former Cubs manager Dusty Baker (from my Chicago days) slowly coming out of the dugout. He puts both hands in his back pockets. He slowly makes his walk to the mound. He is looking down at the grass as he slowly walks, toothpick in his mouth. He gets right up to the mound and just before he greets the pitcher, he turns towards the bullpen, lifts his right arm up, uses his left arm to slap his right forearm, and yells, "Bring in the closer!"

Enter me. I come in and do the exact opposite of whatever that Opener Guy was doing. Most of the time that is easy. Most guys are cordial and gentlemanly. I walk up and confidently ask her a question, usually about our surroundings or her outfit or something like that. Most guys would never dream of touching a girl until they had her permission. I am either grabbing them by the side, or tickling them at the appropriate time, holding their wrist briefly, or making a comment about their unique appearance (a positive one).

Most guys introduce themselves. I never do. Most guys ask what a chick's job is and where she lives. I rarely do. If she is really hot, I try to come off a little cocky. If she is a deer in the headlights (not use to the club scene or being hit on), I play it straight and just try to win her over with my witty personality. If she is sassy, I might bag on some dorky chick's outfit, or some guy's dancing ability, or how bad the DJ is. It doesn't take long for her to recognize that I am different, exciting, and ready to party.

Understand that every woman is different, and you have to adjust your game depending on what type of woman you are hitting on. With some women they want to be intellectually stimulated. I'll try to show them I am smart and can carry an in-depth conversation. *Then* I will tease them or make a borderline sexual comment or touch them in the right area, etc.

With some women, they just want to party that night; they want someone to grab them and lead them to the party. In all of these situations one thing remains constant. I find some way to exude my sexuality. I find some way to, or attempt to, stimulate her mind *and* her body. Then later I can try to get her to come back to my place and close the deal.

Words have to be spoken to get her home. You can't just pull her out of there caveman style. I usually say, "Man, it's still early, let's go back to my place and hang out," or "Let's go to my place and have a drink," or "Come on Steph, we're going to my place," or "Let's go order a pizza and chill at my place," or "Let's go to the afterparty!" This is an unspoken language that translates to: 'Let's go back to my place and see what happens.' I know, it seems cheesy to say, "Let's go have a drink at my place," but believe it or not, it works. It works a heck of a lot better than "Okay, bye, it was nice to meet you." Girls know the game, they just want you to guide them.

When the bars are closing, or even before closing, coercing your girl back to your place is mandatory. You don't know how many times I will be thinking "Geez, how am I going to get this girl back to my place?" I tell myself I have to say *something*. Not trying is not an option. Maybe I throw out there, "Let's keep the party going. Let's go back to my place." You'll be amazed how often it works.

## 24. Be Spontaneous

Spontaneity is at the foundation of meeting women. Acting on impulse is simply the very best way to meet women. You will crash & burn, often, if you rehearse or plan out encounters with women. Women love spontaneity. Make it a part of your game. This is a sure-fire way to get a woman thinking about you, and that is the first step towards attraction. Spontaneity is also a sign of wit and intelligence. Spontaneity shows you have a good sense of humor. Spontaneity is a sign of confidence.

There are a million ways to be spontaneous. Walk down the street and see a beautiful babe and just change direction and approach her. Make eye contact in a bar with a cute girl, then go right over and say Hi. Compliment a complete stranger in the subway, at the grocery store, or in the gym. She will appreciate your impulsiveness. She knows it takes balls to go in cold like that. Spontaneity works just about anywhere.

You can also be spontaneous *after* you meet a chick in a bar. After talking to her for a while, suddenly grab her by the hand and say, "Come with me to get a drink," and pull her away. Just the fact that you are being a man and calling the shots like that is enough to stimulate her attraction. It also separates her from her friends so now you can have an isolated conversation. The spontaneity will be exciting to her. Spontaneity is definitely important in the art of seducing women.

I was at this nightclub with my buddy Johnny. We had just arrived so we were trying to pound down a couple cocktails as we surveyed the playing field. A few feet away there was a couple, one guy and one girl, and you could tell it was a first or second date (never bring a date to a nightclub.) You could just tell when a guy and girl are together but they haven't slept together yet. They were standing an uncomfortable distance away from each other and they just looked awkward together.

Anyway, the girl was fumbling through her purse looking for something. She accidentally turned her purse completely upside down and the entire contents came falling out. Shit was everywhere! It was a big purse too. Some lipstick rolled over to me, so I picked it up and started to help clean up. I was a little intoxicated already and immediately thought of a good, spontaneous idea.

I had four condoms in my back pocket. I took the four gold Magnums out of my back pocket. Discreetly, I tossed them towards the far side of the pile of crap on the ground. Her and her guy were putting stuff back in the purse so they didn't see me do this. Then they crouched back down to clean up more stuff. So that they could both see me, I reached down all the way across the pile of stuff, while they were watching, and picked up the bright gold condoms and handed them to her.

"Those aren't mine!" she shrieked.

She was wiggling her hands back and forth and kind of freaking out.

I saw her date's eyebrows rise as I was handing her the condoms. He must have been thinking "Damn, this chick rolls out with *four* condoms. I don't know if that's good or bad!"

She tried to calm down, "Those are not mine."

"Are you sure?" I said. I shrugged my shoulders. "Okay I'll keep em."

They finished cleaning up the purse mess. The whole thing lasted just a minute or two. I knew Johnny was watching. They walked away and Johnny gave me a side five and we cracked up hard. He said, "That was great dude!!!"

We were both laughing our asses off.

Out of nowhere, some chick shoved me and grabbed my wrist and said, "Holy shit that was hilarious!!!"

This chick was a bad-ass. She had a tattoo on her arm and a tongue ring. Dark hair and a black outfit. She was pretty damn hot. I found out later she was bi-sexual. Anyway, apparently she had watched the whole thing from their table and thought it was hilarious that I tried to say the condoms were that girl's.

This chick really thought I was funny. She and I hung out for a while. We were making each other laugh and buying each other beers and shots. It was cool. I liked it because I thought she was hot and I can never meet chicks with tattoos and tongue rings even though I would like to. We ended up going back to her apartment for a late night hook up. She had her way with me. And it was all from that spontaneous act of throwing the condoms out there.

Here's another good one. Take a random, unplanned trip with a girl. This is the ultimate form of spontaneity.

I was dating this blond girl Kelly for a few weeks. She was a real dreamboat, barbie-doll type chick; innocent, well mannered, private-school educated, strong family support, not slutty, etc. She still lived in the suburbs, right near her parents. I had only banged her once. She was always apprehensive about hooking up with me. I needed to take her out of her element.

She came over to my house on a Saturday afternoon. I said to her, "Let's go to Vegas."

She said, "When?"

"Right now," I replied.

She was the type of person that needed to plan out vacations six months ahead of time. I was not. We got in my car and went to the airport. No luggage, no nothing. I bought two 1-day flights to Vegas. It was expensive, but I had just won a bunch of money playing poker. As we boarded the plane I could tell that she was a little distressed. We went to Vegas and got some cocktails. We popped from casino to casino partying, laughing and having a great time. I got a cheap hotel room on the strip and we had sex all night long.

Went home the next day. That chick went from being stringent and reserved to being totally whipped on me! The spontaneous trip worked perfectly.

One more. My buddy Hoss and I went on a date with these two chicks in San Francisco. We had met them a couple weeks prior. They were both from Sacramento. I met my chick at this nightclub 1015 Folsom in SF. I hooked up with her and she went down on me in the corner of the club near the end of the night. She was blond and slutty, mid 20s, lived in Sacramento. She was hanging on me all night when we met. We were in Frisco so there were numerous gay dudes around, and I was skeptical at how quickly this chick was already so into me. I've seen dudes who look like chicks, so I checked for balls.

*Point of Advice: Anytime there is the smallest of doubts in your mind that your girl might not be a girl, you need to check for balls. Just one mishap and you will be scarred for life. This happened to a close friend; don't let it happen to you.*

I checked for balls. She was definitely a chick. Whew!. She was pissed at me for doing that, but she got over it. Like I said, she gave me hummer later on in the corner. No happy ending, but it was still nice.

Hoss hit it off with her friend that night so we scheduled a night to go out in SF again a couple weeks later. Double dates are always fun, especially with young sluts. We met them in SF and hung out with them a sufficient amount of time until it was time to head back to the hotel room.

My chick and I didn't make it to the room. We had sex in the hotel hallway near the coke machine. This was one horny girl.

We finally got into the room and into bed. Hoss and his chick were pretending to be asleep, but I could tell they were fooling around under the blankets.

My chick got horny again. I obliged her by easing her head down lower so she could give me some head. She did. (I noticed Hoss and his chick peeking out of the blankets watching and giggling.) My chick was excellent at giving head, a real trooper with perfect technique of jacking the shaft and bobbing up & down at the same time. I was rock hard in no time. I knew it would be tough to cum again just from a bj, so I flipped her over and started giving it to her missionary.

I was up on my knees having sex with her. I was having a good ole time when for some reason I felt the impulse to start singing '*Eye Of The Tiger*' by Survivor. I had just watched a Rocky rerun that morning, and I love that song. At first I was just hitting it, normal sex. Then I really started pumping this girl, bodies were slapping loudly. I was singing and getting louder, "*It's the eye of the tiger, it's the thrill of the fight! Rising up to the challenge of our rivals....*" I am a terrible singer but I didn't care. I put both her legs in the air spread eagle, held her ankles, and continued to pump her hard. I was singing loudly and off key, "*...went the distance now I'm not gonna stop! Just a man and his will to surviiiiiiiiive.*"

I looked at her and was thinking how great this song was. I stopped singing and concentrated. It was so hard to finish because I was running on empty. But Rocky wouldn't have quit, so I wasn't quitting. It took everything I had, but I finally climaxed. All over her. It was awesome.

She went to the bathroom to clean up, came back and got in bed. She was all over me. She was cuddling up next to me and nuzzling on my ear. She whispered in my ear, "No one has ever done me like that," as she shyly giggled. My spontaneity had worked too well! It was turning this chick into a Level 3 Clingon.

A half hour later Hoss started singing Eye Of The Tiger. He wasn't having sex. He was just making fun of me. He and his girl started laughing, then I laughed and my girl laughed. It was kind of funny. Then just for fun I had my girl go down on me again. Then Hoss started laughing again.

## 25. Sense Of Humor

Making a woman laugh is much easier said than done, but if you can use your sense of humor and make her laugh, you'll be in like Flynn. Making a girl laugh is the #1 way to attract the opposite sex. Get her laughing and you are on your way to hooking up! Being creative and developing your sense of humor should always be a top priority.

There are so many ways to exhibit your sense of humor; it's difficult to offer guidance on being funny. Here's a quick example. I was at this swanky Japanese lounge, Japonais, in Chicago. We were talking to two good-looking upscale cougars. We were letting them do the talking, trying to judge what type of cougars they were. (They could have been golddigger cougars, married-on-vacation cougars, local horny cougars, newly divorced cougars, or cocktease cougars. We needed to find out.) Sure enough they eventually come out with, "So what do you guys do?" They were indeed golddigger cougars. Right away Johnny told them he was an attorney (he was an options trader), Bucky said he was a stuntman (he was a photographer), and I said I was a chef. These two chicks mulled it over full a couple seconds. They asked Bucky about his job. He told them he was in town shooting a new movie, but he couldn't talk much about it; he had signed a confidentiality agreement. Good one Bucky. Then the blond turned to me and said, "Oh, where are you a chef at?" In a straightforward, normal, truthful tone, I said, "Boston Market......I'm in charge of side dishes."

I pretended to check my cell phone for messages while my response settled in. I'm sure they were thinking "Geez, does he really work at a fast food restaurant?" Out of the corner of my eye I looked at her and cracked the slimmest of smiles. Her and her friend smiled and began laughing. Then I told her, "Just kidding! I'm an attorney too." (I'm not.) From there on in we had them laughing and all three of us hooked up.

It wasn't anything major, just a simple way of exhibiting a sense of humor. Rigid, straightforward guys with no sense of humor have a tough time building rapport. Integrating your sense of humor into the initial conversation is definitely an important factor in developing attraction.

## 26. Tell Them What They Want To Hear

The unfortunate truth is that 95% of the women you meet, you'll never see them again. Don't be afraid to tell a woman a white lie ~ tell her what she wants to hear.

For example, often times I'll make up a random occupation when a woman asks what I do for a living. I've been known to lie about my age. I might even lie about where I live or what my name is.

My buddy Riki will often say to a girl that we should take his yacht out this weekend. If the girl ever agrees he tells her his boat is 'in the shop.' I have been with my buddy Mark when he says, "Let's go back to my house; I have a huge Jacuzzi with a view of the whole city." Then we get back to his two bedroom apartment. He has a stand-up shower, no jacuzzi, and no view at all. The girls usually react by saying, "Yeah, you got us on that one, now make us a drink."

The night I met my ex-girlfriend, I told her I was five years younger than my true age. On the fourth date I came clean. She shrugged it off. A while back I met this hot waitress in Las Vegas and I could tell she really wanted a boyfriend. I told her what she wanted to hear. I told her I just moved to Vegas. I flew into Vegas once a month for three months before she found out I didn't live there. By then we had banged numerous times and I was getting sick of her.

My buddy Derek will be at the club near closing time. He'll get excited and say, "Girls, I have two huge bottles of Dom Perignon at my condo, chilled, on ice. I have been dying for the right occasion to open them. Let's go back to my place and crack open some expensive champagne! Come on, let's go!" The girls just start walking with him and next thing you know, they are back at his apartment. He sneaks in the kitchen, opens a bottle of $5 dollar Cook's, and brings out the flutes of champagne. He puts on some music, and the party has started.

My buddy Party Scars is even shadier. His girlfriend has a phat condo, huge terrace with a view of the bay. She travels all the time and Scars has the keys to her condo. Scars will tell a chick, "You gotta come see my new condo. I just bought it and it's never been partied in! Let's go!" He brings her back there, bangs, and then kicks her out before morning so the neighbors won't see. He'll douse the bed and couch with his cologne, and vacuum the bed.

## 27. Tell Racy Stories At The Bar

Surprisingly, my crew and I have noticed very good results when we are telling stories about getting laid while hanging out at the bar. When we arrive, we'll naturally head to the bar, grab some drinks, and hang out. Inevitably, our conversation will turn to our favorite subject. Pussy. Somebody will ask about last night or last weekend, and a good story will come forth. The stories are always entertaining, and usually very funny. We'll be laughing and having a good time. And we don't hold back. Women are attracted to our body movements while telling the story, our gestures, and our laughter.

First of all, we are laughing, and girls love guys who are laughing. Second, we are ignoring all the chicks at the bar while we are listening to our stories and getting our drink on. This drives chicks crazy. They must be thinking, 'These guys are having fun without hitting on us.' Women are intrigued and want to be a part of our group. I have seen it many times. Chicks will even approach us and even try to jump in our conversation! They can see we are listening intently and laughing and they can tell we are talking about one of their favorite subjects, sex. Anybody would want to be involved in that type of conversation.

Say Johnny went out last night and brought a chick home. They fooled around on the bed, but she wouldn't put out right away. So Johnny gave up, and she went home. We'll say, "You should have banged her Johnny! She was probably horny." Then I will gently smack the nearest girl on the shoulder and say, "Don't you think he should have tried harder?" She will appreciate being asked for her opinion. She'll throw Johnny in front of the bus and say, "Yes, you should have tried harder Johnny!" Then we'll all bag on Johnny. This chick and her friends will feel a part of our group, and we can go from there.

Let me tell you something, women *love* hearing guys talk about their getting-laid stories. They eat it up. Those chicks will want to hang out with us for the rest of the night. Telling R-rated stories at the bar is great way to attract attention without intentionally trying to attract attention.

Sometimes I will be the one telling the story about getting laid, and a hot chick will force her way into our small group, or make it obvious that she is eavesdropping. I will continue the story about getting laid. She will get all hot and bothered and one of us will pull her in and get her involved. She'll start hanging out with us and, next thing you know, she is the subject of tomorrow's story.

## 28. Say Things Other Guys Won't Say

Say things that other people won't say. I am not afraid to talk openly about any subject with a girl I have just met. I think they find it refreshing to find a guy who is open and down-to-earth. The subject of sex is always a good one. I will talk to a girl about sex, sex partners, masturbation, threesomes, kinky sex; just about anything. Women usually respond quite favorably.

I was at a Cubs game at Wrigley, hanging out in the bleachers with a married buddy. My Scottsdale chick called me on the cell phone from Arizona. She was a former stripper and a real dime piece, such a hot piece of ass. I use to do all kinds of kinky things with her. She was Hungarian, dark blond, with perfect firm boobs. She loved for me to cum on her face. (These chicks are hard to find!)

So I was at the game with my married buddy and I thought it would be funny if I talked to her on speakerphone because I knew he would be shocked at the things I could talk to her about. I like fucking around with my married buddies because I know they all dread being married.

I put her on speakerphone and she was telling me how she misses me and how she misses having sex with me. She was talking in her hot Hungarian accent, "Oh yaa baby I miss your sex is so goowd."

"Elizabeth, I am going to do you real good next time I see you Okay."

"Okay yes baby I like dat!"

Then I said, "Can I cum on your face next time baby?"

She replied, "Oh yeah I like it when joo cum on my face! I want to see joo so badly baby."

My married buddy was taken aback.

I was amused at the open-mouthed expression on his face. I talked to her a couple more minutes and then got off the phone. I was really enjoying how taken aback he was.

I guess there were these two chicks in front of us who were listening the whole damn time and I wasn't aware of it. My buddy whispered to me, "Dude I think those chicks heard everything." I said, "I don't care." An inning later those chicks end up twisting around and start talking to us. It was 80 degrees out, we were drinking beers, watching the Cubs lose, and talking to a hot couple of poptarts from University of Illinois. Now that's a great summer day in Chicago. After the game we went to Hi Tops. After Hi Tops we went to my place. After my place....my buddy went home....very late.

My girl spent the night. She was obviously a kinky girl and thought I was kinky too. I was amazed that this chicks wanted to party with us after hearing that conversation. We would have never gotten that far with those chicks without that phone conversation. So don't be afraid to talk to chicks about sex, or let them eavesdrop on a conversation about sex. Saying things other guys won't say could get you laid.

## 29. Go Out With A Group Of Guys

Go out with a group of guys whenever possible. This isn't easy, because many of your friends will have their own agendas. But if you can, set up nights where there is a group going out.

A group of guys commands attention. Women have an attraction to a group of guys. Going to a bar or nightclub with a group of guys is a great way to get women to notice you. Women love the comradery of a group of friends. They want to be a part of it. Anytime you have the opportunity to join in with 4 or 5 other guys going out, do it. Then once you are there for a little while and made your presence known, you can branch off individually and meet some girls.

Many nights my crew and I will meet up at a friend's house for a little pre-party. All of us will have some drinks, bullshit, maybe watch a ballgame or a UFC fight. The pregame is always a lot of fun, and it puts you in a good mood for the rest of the night. Then we'll hit the club. We'll all walk in, order some drinks, and scout out the hot chicks in our vicinity. Next thing you know, everyone is gone; off trying to meet some girls. The next morning we will be telling war stories and everyone will be like, "Where were you?! I didn't see you all night." Yet we were all in the same place working chicks and having fun. I love rolling out with a good group of guys.

## 30. Wingman Requirements

A key necessity for meeting women is a good wingman. A wingman always makes you look good. No chick wants to meet a guy who's there by himself. A wingman gives you stability. A wingman gives you advice. A wingman can provide you with a second opinion. A wingman can jump on her ugly friend if need be. Or he can jump on her hot friend and make it easier for you guys to take both of them home. A wingman can give you fashion tips like, "Please don't wear that tired-ass striped shirt again bro." A wingman can help your drunk-ass get home after a rough night of partying. A wingman can tell you funny stories about getting laid. A wingman can recommend places to go. A wingman can stick up for you when some chick's boyfriend wants to kick your ass. The need for a good wingman cannot be understated.

The more wingmen you have, the better. You never know when a friend might be busy that weekend, or moving out of town, or he might be forced into Snuggle Lockdown by some chick, etc. Having multiple wingmen is always wise. However, it is hard to find good guys to go out with. Some guys are flaky and unreliable, some guys are natural born cockblocks (nbc), and some guys don't like pussy that much (amazing, I know; but some guys are complacent with no pussy.)

Now you can't really dictate how good of a wingman your friends are; the only thing you can do is to make sure that you, yourself, are a good wingman. The #1 quality in a good wingman is reliability. Just be there for your buddies when they need you. Answer the phone when they call. Don't be a no-show. If you can't make it, call or text and let them know you can't make it. If you can tell your buddy needs some assistance talking to some chicks, jump in there and help. Give honest opinions. Send your wingmen a copy of this book. Just being a solid wingman will rub off on your friends and they will become better wingmen themselves.

I was in San Fran for some training to learn how to trade equity options. I had to move out there for three months - they put me and few other guys up in their corporate apartments. Some of the guys had been there for a few weeks already. I was worried I wouldn't learn the stuff fast enough so I made friends with some of the smarter guys. The smartest guy, Mike from Philadelphia, and I became buddies. Philly Mike was Ivy League educated. He would go on to be a great options trader. He had kind of a big gut, love handles, red hair, glasses, and a crooked smile. He was a very likeable guy, but he didn't score very often with the opposite sex. Looks don't even matter that much, he was just too timid. His only move was the horny caveman move. Chicks could read his desperate horniness a mile away, so they usually turned him down.

I had been in San Fran a few weeks now and already scored a couple times. San Francisco was a goldmine for pussy when I lived there. It was all dot.com geeks and gay guys. I owned the town. A bunch of us went out on a Friday night. I knew this was an opportunity to be a good wingman to my smart buddy. I was on a date the night before with a solid 9. I pummeled her twice, so that made me somewhat less horny than usual and more inclined to be an even better wingman. We went out to Balboa Café and had a few drinks. It was a yuppie bar chalk-full of professional women and sophisticated cougars. There was also a bachelorette party there and we were all flirting with them, but I quickly realized it was a small bachelorette party, so I bailed.

Philly Mike & I saw these two good-looking chicks walking our way, possibly on their way out. As they got close I said, "Ohh honey your sweetness is my weeeeeakness." Don't why I said that cheesy shit, but it made them smile. The instant they smiled I grabbed one of their hands and pulled them in. I introduced myself and then introduced both of them to Mike. Mike was pretty happy about that. Mike was really helping me learn some complicated options stuff at work, so I was hoping I could hook us up with a couple chicks as a thank you to him.

These broads were both 28-year-old lawyers. I could tell it was on because we were the only guys in the bar not wearing suits, *and* these chicks were whispering stuff into each other's ear and then looking at me. Anytime chicks start acting like little school girls, you know it's on. We spent a while hanging out with them. I was hoping Mike would hook up with either one of them. I would have taken either one. They were both pretty good looking, 7s, and they were dressed in knee-high tight skirts and blouses. They looked sexy as hell. Mike talked a little to the brunette with big bombs; I talked to the dirty blond with no boobs but a nice ass. Then we all talked together. We were getting drunk and for some reason I suggested we play the Panty Game.

Todd & I had just invented the Panty Game a couple months before in Newport Beach, and it worked well. In the

Panty Game, you use all your intuition to judge the exact color, fabric, and style of a girl's panties. You use the girl's fashion sense, her personality, the mood she is in, and how horny she appears to be. Based on this, you try to guess what kind of panties she has on. Afterwards, the girls have to guess what kind of underwear you have on. Chicks are more than happy to play this game.

There are three great things about the Panty Game. First of all, it gets everyone talking and laughing. Second, the girls have to show some of their panties to see who wins. Usually chicks show the back of their g-string or something like that, but I've had girls lift up skirts for a peak. That's when you know she's a fun girl! Thirdly, and most importantly, this game is a great way to see what kind of a mood a chick is in. You can tell a lot about a girl from what kind of underwear she wears. If she is wearing something like a black lace g-string, look out! She wants to party *that night*. If she is wearing big green grandma-panties, she wants to go home and feed her cat and curl up with a good book. If she is a young poptart wearing pink cotton briefs, Mmmmm daddy like! If she is not wearing any undies at all, well, I don't know what that means but it turns me on like fricken crazy every time I've seen it!

So the four of us were having a great time in this bar playing the Panty Game. The one I was talking to had on leopard-skin g-string underwear. Oh snap! I knew that was a good sign. The other girl had on white sexy briefs. It was hard to interpret those undies. We quickly found out. We were all having a great time when the brunette tells us she has to get going because she has work to do tomorrow. Lame! She leaves and the three of us have another cocktail. I got the sense that it was time to close (attempt to close) so I said, "Let's get out of here." She nodded yes and Philly Mike nodded yes. There are two parts to getting a chick home: getting her to leave, and getting her to come back to your place. I was half way there. I had her saying yes, so after another sip of my drink I said, "Let's go have a drink at my house, I have a great view." I had no view, but I would worry about that later.

This was crossroads. I made that suggestion nonchalantly like I didn't care, but I knew the importance of her response. Her saying, 'Okay' would make this a great night. Her saying, 'No I'm going home,' would make this a worthless night.

She said Okay.

We all went back to my studio apartment. It was right under the Bay Bridge. A tiny studio with no view, but great location. Oh well, she didn't mind. I made three vodka sodas, hers with more alcohol of course. Mike turned on my CD player and the Barry White song I was banging to the night before still was playing, "Can't get enough of your love babe." Perfect.

Studio apartments suck. However, there is one good thing about them. Chicks have nowhere to sit but your bed. That makes it less work when trying to hook up. Mike sat on my recliner. My girl and I sat on the bed. Forget the small talk; I started kissing her after only a few minutes. We were making out passionately and rubbing on each other. I took my shirt off and took her top off to reveal her matching leopard-skin bra. She wouldn't let me take that off though - she was probably self-conscious about her mosquito-bite boobs. One thing led to another. She was still sitting on the bed and I had my pants down so I just went for it. I stood up on my knees and attempted to put my cock in her mouth. This was a daring move, but I had nothing to lose and everything to gain. She was a good girl. A good girl because she started giving me a hummer! Woooohooo!

I had forgot that Philly Mike was even in the room. After a while, I remember looking over at him. He pointed at her and mouthed the words silently, "She's sucking your dick!" He was thrilled. I remember thinking, "Oh, is she *really* Mike? Thanks for pointing that out!?" I liked it that he was so flabbergasted.

She wouldn't take her pants of no matter what, so I knew that a bj was it. Her non-boobs really didn't turn me on. My chick from the previous night was so much hotter. I decided to wingman my bro. Mike was pretty amused by the fact that some chick was giving me head who we had just met a few hours ago. Apparently, he has never seen such a thing. I looked over at him and motioned for him to come over and get a blowjob from her too. He was confused and I knew he was thinking, 'Are you crazy Bill?! There is no way she will suck my dick; she likes you.'

We both knew that she might flip out if someone else tried to get involved. I thought it was worth the risk. Plus, I have a keen sense for shady chicks. This chick was being shady by giving me a hummer with my red-headed buddy sitting there watching. That's a little risqué.

Mike came over. While she was giving me head, I silently gave him hand signals to take his boxers off and shove his cock in her mouth. I moved out of the way but kept petting the top of her head. She saw my dick leave and another dick pop in front of her face. She just took the new dick and started sucking it. Great! I love chicks who love giving head. I backed out and put my boxers on and went over to the kitchen. I looked over and Mike looked up at me and pointed down and mouthed silently, "She is sucking my dick!!" He was so happy. Then the smile quickly faded from his face and he looked down on her. He started concentrating and enjoying the blowjob.

I dug in the fridge for some food. He had a happy ending and she gave us her number and we made plans to go out in a couple nights. That never materialized though.

Let me tell you something, if you ever want to earn somebody's friendship, hook him up with a hummer from a cute girl. After that night, Philly Mike would have laid down in traffic for me. He went on to help me out considerably with work, and the dividends from that friendship continue to pay off - another benefit of being a good wingman.

## 31. Late Night Wingman

We all know that scoring every night is an impossibility. If the night is dragging on and the chances of you scoring look bleak, be a bro and help out your wingman if need be. He might need you to be there so he can hook up with one chick while you babysit her friend. Being a good wingman late night is the right thing to do. Down the road, the favor will be returned. And you never know what will happen late night.

I was at this swanky nightclub in Chicago last summer with my buddy Greg. He was talking to a couple chicks, a tall hot brunette in a short white skirt and her friend. The friend was decent, probably a 6.5 or 7. This club was crackin though - there were hot chicks everywhere so I wanted to find a smokin hot chick for myself. I left Greg and wandered off. We didn't see each other again for a couple hours.

Greg was still talking to the same chicks when I came back. Greg looked like he was in for sure with the hot one. It was late, we were all sauced, the place was closing soon, so I decided to be a good wingman and jump in there and talk to the other one so Greg could isolate his chick and hopefully close the deal.

I was bullshitting with the other chick for about 30 minutes. I was saying anything to this chick because I didn't really care. I was being very flirtatious, grabbing her on her side, briefly tickling her, talking dirty to her; she was loving it. She had brunette hair, kind of bowl haircut, cute face, and really big calves like she was a gymnast or something. She was wearing a black knee-high business skirt and a navy blue low cut top.

The place was closing and Greg was trying to get his chick to come home with him. She declined that offer, but suggested we all go eat somewhere. We all piled in Greg's Chero-kee.

Greg popped in some 50 Cent "*If I Can't,*" and every-thing was going good. The chicks eventually decided on El Presidente Mexican food on Ashland Ave. It was a late night sit-down Mexican food restaurant. In the car on the way I was laughing in the back seat with the 7, can't remember what about, but I remember grabbing her on her side to make her laugh more. We were definitely hitting it off.

We arrive at the restaurant and walk in. It must have been around 3 or 4am. The place was empty. Greg and his girl head for a table and my chick heads for the bathroom. I decided to follow her. She walks in the bathroom and I walked right in behind her. She didn't mind. This bathroom was a real hole. It was very small, maybe 4 feet by 5 feet square. I grab my girl and start kissing her passionately. While we're kissing, the slow door finally eases shut. It became pitch black inside because neither one of us bothered to turn the light switch on. We were making out like it was the last kiss in the world. Total drunk sloppy kissing. I was feeling up her shirt, and be-ginning to unbutton my fly. I got my jeans unbuttoned while still keeping the kissing going. Then I whipped my pig out and grabbed her firmly by the waist. I quickly twisted her around so she was facing the opposite direction. I lifted up her soft black skirt. She was Okay with all this - it was all happening very fast. I pulled her panties to the side, and I mean all the way to the side. I have learned from experience that just moving them to the side leads to them getting in the way and that is very frustrating. The panties need to be stretched all the way over the left cheek. So I get them over the cheek and she graciously bends over. I slipped it in. She was all wet down there so it slid in perfectly. I was about 70% hard to start off, but immediately went to 100% once I started giving it to her. Man, it was good! Nice wet pussy.

I was banging her and her head was hitting the wall ev-ery time because we were in such cramped quarters. We were going at it pretty good. I was in heaven. I was banging away. Her head was hitting the wall on every thrust but she didn't care. Everything was going good when suddenly the door opened and the light switch went on and the fat little Mexican waitress walked in. She thought nobody was in there because the lights were not on. She didn't see us at first. Then she saw us and let out a loud Latin yelp. "Ooooii !"

She looked afraid. She pulled the door shut and waddled away.

That interruption wasn't going to stop me. I bent my girl back down again and started going at it once more. Now the lights were on and I could see! This chick had a nice body and nice ass and I was really getting turned on. No fat anywhere, which was surprising. It's rare when a late night hook up isn't chubby somewhere. I started to get worried that I wasn't going to have time to finish so I started going pretty hard. Her head kept hitting the wall and she was trying to turn her head to the side so it wouldn't hit the wall so hard. This went on for a little while, and I was sweating profusely. I would love to say I had a happy ending but I was hammered and it was just too difficult to finish. She stood up straight and I knew it was time to get out of that hot-box bathroom.

It was still one hell of a good bang session. I don't remember what she said, but it was along the lines of we should go find our friends. I muttered yes, zipped up, and walked out.

It took her more time to come out.

I went straight to our table and sat down across from Greg and his chick and asked, out of breath, if they ordered yet. I was checking my pockets for food money when I looked up at them. They were both staring at me with their mouths open with dumbfounded looks on their faces. I then realized what I must have looked like to them. I was completely disheveled. My hair was all messed up, my clothes were all twisted around, I had lipstick on my face, I was breathing heavily, and sweat was running down my face like I had just run the Boston Marathon.

I looked at them and kind of half-smiled.

"What?" I said innocently.

Greg's look of amazement slowly started to change to a smile as he realized what had just happened. Then his chick saw him starting to smile and she began to understand what had just happened. She did not smile. She was shocked at her friend's behavior.

Her friend came out and had a seat at the table. (I still didn't know her name). We all ordered and ate Mexican food. I was hungry! We tried to make small talk but Greg's chick was freaked out and didn't want to talk. We left soon after. On the way to their place I was hoping Greg & I would be invited in, but Greg's girl was not going to let that happen. Prude bitch.

As soon as they got out of the car and we drove off Greg looked at me and said, "No way!! Did you? Did you?!!?!"

I said, "I did."

That was just good karma for being a good wingman.

## 32. Cockblocks

A cockblock is the lowest form of male species. A cockblock does stupid things that makes hot and horny girls run away. Very simply, a cockblock is a guy who prevents other guys from getting laid. He might be overbearing. He might be too aggressive. He might jealous. He might be mean. He might be in a bad mood. He might smell. He might be gay. He might be attention starved. He might be ignorant. He might be stubborn. He might not understand body language. He might be so horny he acts like a caveman. There are millions of ways a guy can cockblock. If one of these guys are in your crew, you need to set him straight. Cockblocks really piss me off.

Be careful not to cockblock yourself. I have seen guys ruin great opportunities when it is unmistakable that chicks want to hook up. I saw my buddy CC flatly turn down an open invitation to a threesome simply because he didn't realize the girls wanted to party.

CC is my buddy from college. He was on the baseball team. He has blondish hair, baby blue eyes, and wholesome good looks. He could be a real lady killer if he wanted to. CC's real name is Lyle. Dabert and I starting calling him CCTD because he Couldn't Close The Deal if his life depended upon it. That was eventually shortened to CC.

CC was at the bar, innocently ordering a drink. Two chicks sitting in barstools initiated conversation. In no time at all he was totally *in* with these chicks. They were staring at him when he wasn't looking. They were making subtle hints about their single status. The martinis they were drinking were taking affect. They started talking about going home and jumping in their Jacuzzi. They were mentioning things like, "It's a big Jacuzzi; three people could easily fit in there. It's hidden, so nobody can see what goes on in there." Then they would smile at each other. Then they would stare at CC. CC would then say something like, "It might get cold later or too windy for a Jacuzzi." Are you kidding me?! These girls were practically inviting him to get naked & naughty. CC wasn't reading the signs. CC was naïve. He was cockblocking himself. I think he got one of the broad's phone numbers and nothing ever came of it. If a girl is giving you hookup signs, you gotta follow through!

I was at the nightclub Rain in Las Vegas a while back. I had lost my buddies. I was solo, drinking a Kettle One/Red Bull, leaning on the stairs wall, just chillin. Some chick comes up and blindsides me. She says, "Chris! Where is everybody?" I respond "I don't know. I can't find *anybody*!"

Keep in mind my name is not Chris. I could have cockblocked myself in this situation, but I just went with it. We got a couple more drinks and hung out for a while.

After twenty minutes, I thought I might possibly be *in* with this chick. She was Jewish, dark hair, nice rack, tight jeans. I had nothing to lose, so I put my hand on the side of her neck and went in for a kiss. We started making out. She was surprised. The second we pulled away she said, "Chris! I wasn't expecting that." I said, "Well I just felt the moment." She smiled.

A little while later I conned her into going up to my room at the Palms. My excuse was to check and see if any of 'our friends' were up there.

I was so curious how this chick thought she knew me, but I knew if I asked I would be exposed. We left the club and took a short elevator ride to my room upstairs. We were making out a little and I was trying to coerce her into a blowjob. After more than a dozen fricken "No's," I finally got her to give me a bj before we left to go look for our friends. That many Nos were so damn annoying. She gave me a half-ass blowjob too. She was constantly starting, then stopping, then whining, "Come on Chris, let's go downstairs."

Bitch, just suck my dick.

That's what I was thinking. But not what I was saying.

"Come on baby, just one more minute. I'm almost there. Come on baby."

More stopping, starting, whining....

Finally, a happy ending. Whew!!

We went back downstairs. I was in a great mood now and wanted to party! OWWWWW!!!! It was still early too! Her cell phone rang and I got a little worried. I could hear her friend bellow out like a drunk sorority girl, "Where are yooooou!? We are all at Spearmint Rhino! Come meet us here!"

I overheard my girl say, "Okay! We'll be right there... Guess who I just hooked up with!?" She smiled. The other bimbo said, "Whoooooo?!" With a happy smirk on her face my chick said, "Chris! Him and I will be right there!" and she hung up the phone.

I was relieved not to be busted. This was a sticky situation. It was now time for me to split. This girl really wanted me to come with her, but I wanted to cut this broad loose. I wasn't that into her for saying No to me so many times, and things could get awkward when I show up and the real Chris is there. She pleaded with me to come with her. After some quick thinking, I told her I left my credit card at the bar and I would meet her there. She didn't like that idea, but she agreed.

Man, I wish I could have been there to see her telling her sorority friends that she just hooked up with Chris and gave him a blowjob. They would look all puzzled and tell her Chris has been with them the whole time.

I am glad I didn't cockblock myself in that situation.

## 33. Work The Help

Always love to work the help. Flirt with hot bartenders. Flirt with waitresses. Flirt with flight attendants, bank tellers, blackjack dealers, and so on. A chick usually has her guard down while she is working. This is a great time to make a good first impression. Then when you come back a second time, it's like you are friends. Then a third time, if you are getting a good vice, she is ready to be asked out.

Some waitresses and bartenders are ready to party that night. I've hooked up with bartenders late night after they get off. After they've done a shot or two behind the bar, they want to party. I have pulled waitresses out of sushi restaurants when my crew & I go for sushi. It's simple. I just say, "You should come meet us out tonight." Restaurants usually close early enough for chicks to party that night.

Another great place to work the help is strip joints. The waitresses at strip joints are always easy to talk to. Show some true interest in them, instead of the slutty strippers. They'll be flattered with the attention. Strip club waitresses separate themselves from the strippers, and they don't mind proving they are better than the strippers by agreeing to party with you after work.

Strippers themselves are easy targets too. Anytime I go to strip club, I am trying to pull the girl out of there. I'm not blowing my money on them like regular customers, I am inviting them to party with us. Strippers love to party and can often be persuaded to come out after work.

Another group I love to flirt with are the women behind the airline counters. Those chicks love to flirt. If she is cute at all, I will stand by the side of the kiosk while she helps all the other customers, chat and flirt with her. When it's time for the upgrade baby, you know I am sitting pretty. I have been upgraded on a number of flights, and dated a number of chicks I have met at the airport.

There is only one place I will never work the help - my favorite watering hole. It's the place my buddies and I frequent the most often. I always pull tail out of this place. This nightclub/bar, (I won't reveal the name and ruin it) is like fishing in a barrel.

I won't work the help there because, first of all, the bartenders hate me. They despise me.

I take it as a compliment that the bartenders there hate me so much. All of the bartenders are hot chicks. They see me, night after night, pulling pussy out of that bar. It must piss them off for some reason. They give me shitty service and dirty looks all the time. I have made an ass out of myself at this place a number of times too. I will be leaning against the bar drunk, sloppily making out with some chick. Then I will take her home. I'll be back there the very next night doing the same thing with a different broad.

What makes this joint so good is that it has a constant influx of out of town and suburbs chicks, and a lot of local naïve poptarts. It's a goldmine. It is dark, and they usually play really good hip hop.

I have had my dick sucked on the dance floor there before, in the corner. Twice. I have been with a chick by the bar and pulled her knockers out and sucked on them. That happened twice also. Some chick with a big diamond ring on her left hand talked to me at the bar for fifteen minutes. Out of nowhere she grabbed and we started making out. We kissed for a good ten minutes. Ooooh, the bartenders hated that one.

I have stood with my back leaning against the bar, drinking a beer, while a young college girl with too much alcohol in her system bends over, puts her hands on the ground, and grinds her ass on me dancing like a hoochie mama from a MTV video. Then I take her home.

I make out with chicks all the time at the bar, lick their faces, squeeze their asses, all kinds of shit. I was talking to some chick in a short, one piece, lightweight, sexy pink cloth skirt. I talked her into taking her panties off and giving them to me. This little poptart reached up under her skirt and took her panties off and gave them to me as a gift right there, right in front of two hot bartenders. Then I sloppily made out with her as I held her g-string in my hand for the bartenders to see. Yes, I antagonize them a little bit. Those bartenders and waitresses really don't like me. The bouncers and doormen think I am a legend. That is the only place I don't work the help. Everywhere else, working the help is a good idea.

# II. Pre-Bang

# 34. "I'm Not Going to Sleep With You Tonight"

I can't tell you how many times I have heard, "I'm not going to have sex with you; I just met you." Other variations of this statement include: "I'm not going to do anything with you tonight." or "Listen, I just want you to know, I am not going to sleep with you tonight." or "I'll go home with you, but nothing is going to happen."

What is truly amazing about this declaration is how delusive it is. I get laid just about every time I hear this! It is money in the bank! Almost every time I have heard a woman say "I'm not going to sleep with you," I sleep with her. We bang. That night. I go home with the girl, one thing leads to another, the girl throws in the obligatory "no" a few times, then she throws in a "We shouldn't," then we are be-bopping naked and getting freaky all night long.

Now that I have become so well educated on this phenomenon, I start salivating like Pavlov's dog as soon as I hear the declaration. I know I am about to score! I will be partying with a chick. It will be getting late. I will say to her, "Why don't we go have drink at my place?" She replies, "Okay, but I want you know, I am not going sleep with you or anything like that." I give myself a mental high five and say to myself, 'Cool, I'm getting laid!'

Don't ask me the psychology behind it; I just know it works. My best guess is that the woman is considering sleeping with you. She knows she will feel guilty in the morning, so she is actually telling *herself* that she is not going to sleep with me. She hopes she has enough will power to adhere to her own instructions. She realizes most guys probably believe her when she makes this declaration and therefore, they never try anything. If she really had no intention of sleeping with you, she wouldn't even bring it up! She is bringing it up because she *is* considering it!

Here is my translation of, "Listen, I am not going to sleep with you tonight." Woman: "Listen guy, I've had a great time with you so far. I want to go home with you and get naked and get fucked silly, but I need to be coerced and mentally massaged and talked into it. That way I can justify my slutty actions." I have no problem adhering to her wishes.

## 35. "But I Don't Even Know You"

This statement is whole different story. This line is a true road block, and not easy to overcome. As you progress in sharpening your skills with women, you will undoubtedly hear this line from a girl you are trying to score with: "But I don't even know you," or "But we just met," or "We shouldn't; we barely know each other."

Man, when you are trying to close the deal, this statement is a real bummer!

It's difficult to overcome, but not impossible. When you hear this line you have to pull out all the stops and say *anything* you can to overcome this obstacle. Just know the most important thing: she does want to party! She is saying this because she does indeed like you - she wants to proceed with hooking up, but she doesn't want to feel bad about it the next day. And she doesn't want to lose your respect by hooking up too soon. It is your job to make her feel like this will last, and that you & her have a connection. You have to say caring and nurturing things like, "I know, but we've gotten to know each pretty well in this short time, and that's a good sign."

I might say this, "Yes, we just met, but we are going to be seeing a lot of each other, I can tell." Another good response is, "All I know is I like you and you should do what you want." Another money closer I use is, "A month from know we'll be having sex all the time and laughing that we didn't have sex tonight. We might as well enjoy this moment." A last resort is, "It's better to regret something you've done instead of regretting something you haven't done."

Why does a girl say, "But I barely know you?" She is simply looking for positive reinforcement that you two are going to see more of each other, that you are a standup guy, that you are not just a horny caveman. This is tough because most of us are just horny cavemen.

## 36. Nice Guys Finish Last

The myth is indeed true. Nice guys finish last. The nice guy routine is played out man! Nice guys at the bar might get a phone number at best. She might even classify you as 'a friend' and then you'll *never* get any action. Being edgy or acting aloof makes you desirable because attractive women are accustom to being treated like royalty by most other shmucks. Many women are attracted to bad boys. They are unlike other guys who kiss their ass all the time.

A good example of this theory occurred last week. Since I have been writing this book, I have been *en fuego*. I think all of the skills and wingman tips I have are coming to the forefront. I definitely have my A-game going. I've been hooking up left and right. In the middle of hot streak for sure. I currently have four very hot pieces of ass in my rotation. The only one who wasn't putting out was this hot blond model I have known for a month or two. I almost closed it the first time her and I hung out - had her naked and everything, but I fumbled. Then she put on her chastity belt and wouldn't give it up. I'm sure she has tons of guys that want to fuck her. She is the type of chick that enjoys the attention. Typical stuck up biatch.

Normally I would kick her to the curb. She has an unbelievable body though! So I have kept her around hoping one day she will give it up. I have been out with her a few times. She'll get wasted drunk, flirt with me and cocktease me all night long. Very frustrating. I have been spending a lot more time with the other girls in my rotation, at least they put out. I've been trying to dog her and let her know I am different and I won't put up with this cocktease crap. Every once in a while I'll bootie call her drunk when I know she is sleeping just to show her I don't give a fuck.

Two weeks ago I was out with her and five other friends at this tiny nightclub. It was off the foshizzle packed with hot chicks! My dumbass model broad (who is actually smart and getting her master's degree) gets really drunk. Then she wants to go home. I contemplated leaving with her. She wanted me to. Maybe she would finally put out? I decided to stay and party with all the hot little honeys running around. She left with my buddy Johnny for a ride home. I partied more, made out with a couple chicks, had a great time, and left much later.

On the way out, I called her up and went over to her apartment. Johnny was there passed out in the corner. I think he was hoping to hook up with her. Yeah, we roll like that. Not a big deal. She was on the couch, wasted, watching TV in her panties and bra. I turned off the TV and put on some chillin hip hop, Fort Minor, on her stereo. I started kissing her neck and grabbing her ass, trying to be gentle and caring even though I was horny and drunk. She pushed me away. I leaned back in for some caressing and some soft kisses, and then I and grabbed some more ass.

She gets all fired up and says, "What the hell is your problem?! Is that all you ever want to do is fuck me?! Is that all you want from me?!! Go ahead if that's all you want then asshole! If that's all you want, than go ahead and fuck me!"

Hmmm. The crossroads. We have arrived at the crossroads. Most men take the wrong turn here.

I stripped her panties off, opened up a condom, jumped up on her, stuck my dick in her with no condom, and fucked the shit out of her.

Her head was turned to the side up against the couch and she just let me pummel her. After a good session, I dropped a big yogurt load on her stomach.

She saw that and got pissed. *Really* pissed. "You weren't even wearing a condom?!! You didn't even care to make me cum?!!! You're an ASSHOLE!! Get the fuck out, just get OUT!"

Normally I would stay and try to defend my actions, but I actually *did* want to get out of there. She is really annoying but the hottest chick in my rotation right now. So I said, "Your making me leave? Geez, okay," and I left. Definitely not a nice guy move, but I wanted out of there.

I was out with buddies a few nights ago and she met up with us at a local bar. (She knows my other friends too.) It was college night, $1 bottles of beer, and we were all getting drunk.

I was not surprised when she pulled me aside. She was still mad at me, but I could sense that she wasn't too mad. She explained to me that she's only had sex with seven guys, but dated many, many guys. She said anytime she has been with other guys and blurted out, "Is that all you want to do is fuck me?! Fine! Then go ahead!" that the guy has responded: "No baby, I don't want it to be like that; I care about you...."

They consoled her and crap like that. And they got no love for another month or two. She said she even made one guy wait a whole year. Suckers!!! I did the very opposite of those fools. I was proud of myself. How many guys would have straight up banged her like a cold blooded pimp? Not many.

If you got the go ahead, you better get down to business!

That night at the bar she told me she was so mad at herself for having sex with me. She punched me and acted like she hated me. She was emphatic that she would *never* have sex with me again and that I truly was an asshole.

Not three hours later I was tapping that ass again.

Now she calls me all the fricken time. Like I said, this girl is very annoying, so I dog her most of the time. The more I dog her the more she wants me. Just goes to show, nice guys finish last.

## 37. No Means Yes

Just about every girl I have ever tried to score with has said 'No' to me. And yet I get laid all the time, more than anybody I have ever met. How can this be? The answer is summed up: No means yes. Please do not take this literally, but you should have the mindset that no means yes, or no means to try a little more. Keep on trying to hook up with a girl, in a subtle manner, not by forcing the issue, but through kissing, talking, rubbing, etc.

Every girl in the America feels obligated to say no and act like she doesn't want to have sex. This is an American thing. Women in other countries don't play these games. Go to Europe or South America and you will see what I mean. If a girl wants to have sex with you there, she does. If a girl wants to have sex here in America, she says no. It is just our culture. Once you have an understanding of this philosophy, you can keep up your pursuit and expect the girl to give in after three or four no's.

Many girls feel implored to deny a guy when they are hooking up. Women feel less slutty if they are 'talked into' having sex. Women have a hard time seeing a guy again if they have sex too quickly. Women don't want to be perceived as promiscuous or easy. If they put out right away, they are worried that *you* will think they *always* do that. By them saying 'no' multiple times, they want you to understand this is a rare occasion if they do sleep with you. They feel vindicated if they say no a bunch of times, and then give up the pussy. Quite simply, most women *do* want to have sex, they just want you to think they never have sex this quickly.

I understand this psychology and I use it in my favor.

Occasionally you will run into some icy cold broad and no will actually mean no. You will be able to recognize this though. She will sternly and emphatically say, "No." Or she will say no and get up and leave. Or she will say, "No! And I mean it." Or she will slap you.

All of these make it easy for you to realize this chick does not want to party. So just get out of there and move on. At all other times though, keep up your pursuit and your girl will usually give in.

I was in bed with a girl and she said 'No' over ten times. Ten times! I didn't give up though because she was still giving off signs that she did want to hook up. She loved it when I was playing with her box. And she was giving me a really spirited tug job. She kept telling me how much she liked me and she wanted to see me again. I thought she was cool too, and I wouldn't have minded dating her. Sure enough, something changed and she must have realized, "Geez, I *would* actually like to have sex; I should stop saying no." We ended up getting it on. I don't know what changed her mind, but my perseverance paid off.

I have been with some girls who say no every time, all night long. In the morning I wake up with a stiffy. I give it one more try. She is receptive and horny and we have some great morning sex. She must feel like we waited a sufficient amount of time.

The moral of this story here is to understand women and not give up until you are sure that she doesn't want to fool around. Persevere! No means keep trying!

## 38. Get Naked

When I finally get a girl alone and I am beginning to hook up with her, I always get buck-naked as soon as I can. This is good for a couple reasons. First, it makes a girl more comfortable about removing her clothing. If she is going to be the first one getting naked, she might be apprehensive. Some chicks are shy. Some chicks are uncomfortable about their bodies. Some chicks feel slutty if they are the first ones getting naked. Quash those concerns by taking your clothes off first.

Second, your no-clothes demonstration puts some peer-pressure on her to remove some of her own clothing. She should feel a little dumb fully clothed while you are buck-naked, at least that's how I look at it. If they are on the fence about removing their clothing, say this, "Let's get under the covers first." Then pull the comforter up over them. Then go in for some more kisses, and while you are kissing, get her shirt off and then the bottoms. Then you are golden.

As soon as I get in bed with a chick, I remove my shirt immediately. During the next few kisses I am grabbing her boobs and slipping my pants & boxers off at the same time. I don't mess around man. I get right down to business.

This definitely works most of the time. Yeah sure, chicks are sometimes surprised to see me naked on the bed after the first kiss, but I just say, "Yeah, I love to be naked." One out of twenty will freak out and run away and never call you again. So what! Most will respond positively. After all, they are in bed or on the couch or in their parents car with you right? They want to hook up too!

## 39.  Use Any Privacy Available

Guys often underestimate the resources available for hooking up. Men assume the only way they can get laid is at home in their bed. Not so.

Use any privacy available to hook up. Often times you will find yourself with a chick and she is ready to go. 'Ready to go' meaning she is feeling just as passionate and daring as you are. Most guys are patient and will try to get her home to a bedroom, or even worse, wait until the third date. Ugghh! I disagree with this. Waiting can make a girl change her mind, or sober up, or get tired, or she might remember she has boy-friend, etc.

There is nothing wrong with finding a semi-private place and hooking up with the chick right then and there. I have had sex in many awkward and open venues, including stairwells, elevators, back seats, front seats, dance floors, dark alleys, sleeping bags, concerts, the forest, my office, Taco Bell drive-thru, airplanes (Yes, I am a member of the Mile High Club), parking lots, and many, many bathrooms.

As you can tell from some of my other escapades, I have no qualms about hooking up anywhere, anytime. Nightclub or bar bathrooms are not out of the realm. I have discovered that chicks have no problem entering a bathroom and getting it on. I have had sex or a bj in a number of public restrooms, with girls I have met that day. I can't tell you it's normal because I am still bewildered every time it occurs.

One of the most memorable romps came at a dive bar in downtown San Jose, CA. The bar was called Cinnebar. Every Thursday night Cinnebar played disco. This bar was a real hole. A locals only place. One of those shady, tiny, downtown city bars with no windows you would never walk into. But Thursday nights were different. Thursdays it turned from a small, locals only dive bar, into a small dive bar with hot drunk college chicks dancing to 70s and 80s disco music. The place was cool man.

My buddy CC and I frequented the place often one summer. CC & I had finished college, so we didn't know anybody that went to this bar, but we always had a good time. We were in there getting drunk one time when CC went to the front of the bar to get a cigarette. In the back of the bar they had a DJ spinning 70s disco on a turntable. People danced near the DJ.

I noticed this blond behind me. She had brand new big ole fake tits. She was boogying her ass off to 'I Will Survive.' I knew from experience that when chicks get new boobs, they go hogwild the first couple months.

*New Boobs Phase One - A two month phase occurring immediately after receiving a new boob job. During this phase the female goes hogwild slutty because she can now attract higher level males who previously were not interested.*

I got up, strong-arm grabbed her by the hand and started dancing with her. She loved it, naturally. There wasn't much room to dance in this bar but we were making the best of it. The bar was long and narrow, probably 15 feet wide and 70 feet long, and like I said, it was a real hole. But the music was good! This chick and I were swinging each other around and having a blast.

A couple songs go by and I grab her by the waist, and, since we were now so close to each other, start making out. I'm all for kissing passionately, but this chick was trying to swallow me. She was really drunk or horny or I don't know what. She was kissing and swallowing my tongue and wouldn't let go.

Another song goes by. As we are dancing she comes in real close and we start making out again. I was like, 'Damn, this chick is ready to go.'

We were near the back end of the bar. I pulled her by the hand and walked us straight into the guy's bathroom. I needed to see what would happen if we had some privacy.

There was one pisser and one toilet in this nasty bathroom. No stall or doors, just a square 10x10 bathroom. I pinned her against the side wall and we started passionately making out again. I was feeling up her new rock-hard boobs. They were so damn hard they weren't even fun to play with. I began to unbutton my jeans. My pants fell to the floor. I was going Commando that night (no underwear). I reached down and started unpeeling her black spandex pants and panties.

Up until now, neither one of us had spoken one word to each other. Not on the dance floor, not after the kiss, no introductions, nothing. Totally strange hooking up with a girl without one word being spoken.

My very first words to this girl were about to be spoken. What would they be? What's your name? I think you are hot? Nice to meet you, my name's Billy. No.

In a low, slow voice I muttered my first words, "Grab the sink."

She turned to her side and reached over and grabbed the sink. Good girl.

Her pants were at her knees. I got behind her and worked it in. It was tough getting it in, but I did. I started giving it to her. My first thoughts were, 'Oh man I'm getting laid this is so fuckin awesome!" A few pumps later I started thinking, "Holy shit, this door is not locked, some dude is going to walk in here any second!" I was fricken worried. Bathrooms don't stay empty for long. I couldn't reach the door to lock it, and I sure as hell didn't want to stop doing what I was doing. So I was stuck. I was contemplating stopping and going over to lock the door. Then I thought she might say, 'That's enough,' if I stop. What would you do? Tough call. I said fuck it and I kept boning her.

Another minute goes by. I was just starting to enjoy the sex. Suddenly, the door swings open and some dude walks in.

I was mortified.

Talk about getting caught with your pants down. There were probably 50 or 60 guys in that bar. I only knew one of them. But who walks in? CC!! CC randomly walks in to take a piss! I was so relieved it was him and not some stranger.

I will never forget his reaction. He walked in and the first thing he saw was my white ass. His first reaction was he looked away. Nobody wants to see some dude's white ass in the mens room. Immediately, he snapped his head back towards me. His mouth dropped open. He saw it was me. He saw this blond chick bent over the sink getting railroaded by yours truly.

CC was frozen. He was in disbelief. I could see the wheels turning as his eyes tried to tell his brain what he was seeing. His look of astonishment was priceless! He was so shocked he couldn't even smile back at me. I'll never forget him trying to comprehend the situation. I had probably seen him 15 to 18 minutes ago when we were both sitting on barstools drinking cocktails. In that amount of time I had met a random chick and was now boning her in the mens bathroom.

It was so funny watching him try and figure out what to do. He didn't know whether to take his piss, walk back out, or talk to me and ask me what the hell was going on.

He didn't say a word. He just turned around and walked out like a robot.

This blond girl was losing interest. We both pulled our pants back up. Once again I didn't get to finish. Dammit! We walked out. CC, being a good wingman, was outside the door holding up the rest of the line. She went over to her friends and I went with CC over to the bar to get a couple beers. CC was still in disbelief. The first thing he said to me was, "Tell me you know that chick." I said "I don't even know her name." His mouth dropped open again.

A few minutes later I went over to the blond girl and hung out with her for a while. Surprisingly, she wasn't freaked out by what had occurred in the bathroom. I could overhear her friend saying to her, "Why were you in there?! Are you Okay?!" and she was replying, "I know what I was doing. I wanted to do it, leave me alone."

Her friends didn't know she was going through New Boobs Phase 1. Regardless, I went home with her that night and boned her all night. But I never saw her again after that.

## 40. Many Times Phone Numbers Lead To Nothing

Understand that no matter how good you are at picking up women, phone numbers rarely lead to getting laid. The best playboys in the world might get four or five phone numbers in a week; three of those chicks won't return the phone call. One or two might, but nothing ever materializes. That is just the cold hard facts and you shouldn't let it bother you when a chick doesn't return your phone call.

Women give their phone number out all the time. They know that if they answer the phone or return the phone call, they will be asked out on a date. First dates suck. Therefore, it's easier for the woman to just avoid the whole situation by ignoring the phone call.

I have developed a new policy of only calling a chick once. If she doesn't answer or return that phone call, I throw in the towel. There are plenty of other chicks out there. If this chick was interested at all, she would have called back. You can't get a chick to call you by calling her more often. Calling her often makes you look desperate.

*Point of Advice: The first phone call. Never call a chick more than once. Calling her two or three times makes you seem desperate or weird. Don't be that guy. If you don't hear from her, move on.*

We downplay the importance of phone numbers. Don't spend your time trying to get her phone number, instead, spend your time trying to get her to like you. Guys who's only goal is a phone number end up with a ton of phone numbers and a bad case of blue balls.

Don't get me wrong, getting a phone number always puts me in a good mood. Just don't get discouraged when the phone number doesn't materialize into naked Twister.

## 41. First Phone Call

You have a great night out. You get a cute chick's phone number. All is good. A few days go by. Now it's time to make the dreaded first phone call. Everyone dreads making that first call. And rightly so. If you don't sound cool, or if you say something stupid, most likely you will not get a second chance.

You need to handle this situation like you do every other. You need to exhibit confidence. When making the first phone call, speak very s l o w l y. That is the first tip, and a very important one. Whether she answers or you are leaving a message, speaking slowly will convey self assurance.

Have one or two places in mind to take her *before* you call her. Chicks don't want indecisive guys, and they don't want the pressure of choosing where to go. Guy's who say; "Well, where do you want to go?" are soft. Women want decision makers. So when the conversation comes around to it, say, "I know of Such&Such place, that's where we should go," or "I really want to try Such&Such place. What do you think?" She will appreciate you taking charge of the situation.

Here is another little trick I use when making the first phone call. As we have said, women like spontaneous, confident men. Here is how to make a spontaneous and confident impression when calling. I dial the number and as soon as someone picks up I pretend like I am in mid-sentence talking to someone else away from the phone. For example, I will be calling Jody for the first time; I hear Jody's phone pick up and I will be saying, "Turn down the music bro, that song sucks," or "Yeah I like that song dude," or "Yeah I can be there tomorrow, just fax me the paperwork." It's as if I am unconcerned with the phone call to Jody. Jody answers the phone and hears me talking to someone else. I say, "Oh Jody? Hey this is Billy! What's going on...how are you?" I attempt to time it so she only hears the second half of my sentence to this fictitious person. This has the affect of showing her that I am completely at ease about this phone call. It makes it appear like I called her on a whim; the phone call wasn't planned. It shows her that she is not that important to me. If she was important to me, I would be giving the phone call 100% of my attention, which I am not. She senses that I am relaxed and not nervous about the first phone call. That relaxes her and we usually have a cool conversation.

Anything you can do on that first phone call to seem less rigid and more down-to-earth will increase your chances of seeing her again.

## 42. "I'll Call You Tomorrow"

As soon as you tell a chick you will call her tomorrow, you'll walk away kicking yourself! You'll realize you are now obligated to call. Never say, "Okay, I'll call you Tuesday." Never say, "I'll call you after dinner." Giving a specific time you will call is a rookie move! Instead, say, "I'll call you," or "I'll talk to you soon." My standard is, "Okay, I'll talk to you later." There is no confirmed time. There isn't even a confirmed phone call. The only thing confirmed is that we will talk at some future point in life. It leaves her hanging a bit. It makes her wonder if I am going to call. Also, it leaves the door open for her to call me.

If you just met the chick, you definitely don't want to be calling her the following day. I always give her a few days to wonder if I am going to call or not. This evokes the theory that women love a challenge. Maybe she wasn't that into you. Waiting five or six days to call will make her wonder, "Is that guy going to call me or what? I thought he liked me." Then when you do call she is happy and relieved, and she's probably receptive to being asked out on a date.

## 43. First Dates Suck

Trying to meet chicks, 'the chase,' is always fun. Hooking up with them, of course, is a lot of fun. And hanging out with a cool chick after you have been out together a few times is great too. By then you are totally comfortable with your girl. You can actually show your true personality. You can bang whenever you want, etc.

What have we left out? The dreaded first dates. First dates can make you uncomfortable and nervous. First dates can be a complete waste of time. First dates are a crap shoot - half the time they suck. However, you have to go through with them. It's part of the game. It's the only way to find a chick you enjoy hanging out with. Here are a few first date quick tips to help the situation.

~ When possible, try to avoid taking her to the usual 'date places.' Take her somewhere out of the ordinary. No boring French restaurants.

~ Sporting events are a great place for first dates. The sporting event will shift attention away from the both of you. After the game you guys will be much more comfortable with each other.

~ Do not spend and excessive amount of money on the first date. Do not take her to a super expensive restaurant. Do not go 'over the top' on your first date. This is a huge mistake. First of all, if gives off the wrong impression. It shows that you are trying too hard and care too much about impressing her. She will be just as happy at a mid-level restaurant. Furthermore, there is a good chance you will not see her again after this date! Maybe you don't like her or she doesn't like you, or you're just not hitting it off. Therefore, the expensive restaurant is just a waste of money.

~ Do not take her to the cheapest place in town.

~ Any time you are on a first date and you encounter a homeless guy begging for money, *always* go out of your way to give him a buck or two. I never give homeless bums a nickel because I know they'll just go blow it on booze or cigarettes. But if I'm on a date, that all changes. I always donate some money and smile. Your date will definitely remember this. It will paint you in a good light. This is what she will tell her girlfriends about the next day when they ask her how her date went.

~ If you do hit it off, always go in for a kiss at the end of the night. It might be awkward, but you better man-up and do this or else she might group you in that "nice guy" category and then you won't get laid for months.

~ Never beat off before a date. Contrary to what others say, don't beat your meat prior to seeing girls. You want to have all your testosterone there for the whole world to see. You don't want to be passive. You want that horniness and aggressiveness to come out a little bit in your personality. This will show her you're not there for the tea & crumpets; you are there to eventually get laid. Chicks want masculine men, not passive men.

~ Do not go to a movie on the first date.

~ Do not let her catch you staring at her boobs during the date.

~ Try to get her drunk or a little intoxicated on the date. Order wine if she likes wine. Order cocktails, beers, whatever is appropriate. It will lighten up the mood. Things will go more smoothly.

~ Don't be on the phone all the time during your date. That is just rude. If she is on the phone often during your date, that is not a good sign. Chicks, especially young poptarts, love cell phones and yapping on the phone. You have to give them *some* leeway, but too much cell phone talk is not cool. I was out with one chick on our first date and this hot little poptart was on the phone *all the time*, talking about nothing important. It was really starting to piss me off. Never once did she say to me, "Do you mind?" or "Sorry about that." When dinner came, she was *still* on the phone and I was steaming. Twenty minutes yapping to her damn girlfriends about nothing. I got up to go the bathroom and walked out and left her there. See ya! I'm sure she had to pay the bill and wasn't too happy about that. Now she has something to yap to her friends about.

## 44. Keep Her Guessing

A true gigolo always keeps his girl guessing. A sucker does the opposite; he's rock solid and dependable and boring. Mix up the amount of attention you give a girl. Give her undivided attention for an extended period of time - for an hour, for a day, or whatever the situation demands. Then, next time, be too busy to talk to her or hang out with her. She won't know what to think. This will drive her crazy, and like it or not, she'll be thinking about you. You will be stuck in her head. She will wonder if you like her or not. She will wonder if she did something wrong. She will wonder when you are going to call. This is how the attraction process begins. People are attracted to what they are familiar with. She will be thinking about you so often that this will turn into an attraction. Keep her guessing.

## 45. Act Like You Don't Care

Develop the attitude of not caring. For some reason, this attitude attracts women. Guys who care are simple to figure out. Guys who don't care are mysterious. Acting like you don't care exudes confidence. Acting like you don't care shows that you have complete freedom.

Acting like you don't care shows her that you are not looking for her approval. It shows that you are relaxed. Men who are relaxed in a conversation and not looking for approval subconsciously gain the upper hand. The woman will then revert to small talk in order to keep the conversation going. Then you have taken the first step in getting her attracted to you.

The opposite is also true. Acting like you care a lot, or acting like you are trying to win her approval causes her to lose attraction.

I have acted like I don't care for so long now that I actually don't care. Now that is supreme confidence. In addition, acting like you don't care makes it much easier to approach women. Who cares if she shoots you down? You are tha man. That is the right attitude to roll with. When you go out, act like you don't care.

## 46. Bang First, Then Worry About The Consequences

Always bang her first, and then worry about the consequences. There will be numerous times when you are wondering if you should bang this girl or not. Maybe she works with you, maybe she is pretty ugly but she has great boobs, maybe she is your roommate, your secretary, your teacher, maybe she is your sister's friend, maybe she is your ex-girlfriend who is engaged now, maybe you barely know her. All of these scenarios have repercussions if you hook up with this chick. Well let me give you this advice first hand. Always bang first and worry about it later. I live by this motto and it has almost always been the right decision. Here is why: I guarantee at some point in the future, you will say to yourself, "Damn, I wish I would have banged that chick," or, "Damn! I should have had sex with that girl. What was I thinking?!"

*Point Of Advice: At some later point in life, you will say, "Gosh, I should have had sex with that girl when I had the opportunity." Thus, you might as well go ahead and have sex with her now. Live without regrets.*

It might be a day later when you realize that you passed up a golden opportunity. It might be a week later when you are horny and thinking about her. It might be a year later when you look back and realize that chick really liked you. Personally, I hate that feeling. A wise man (me) once said "It is better to regret something you have done, than to regret something you have not done."

Now sure, a few times it has blown up in my face. Maybe a chick is really uncomfortable working with you after you two have been intimate. Maybe you regret the experience because she was really ugly. Maybe some dude wants to kick your ass for messing with his chick. However, 90% of the time nothing happens and you are glad you banged her.

There can be another scenario. What about when you two have been out on a few dates, but she hasn't put out yet? That is the worst. Banging her asap is of paramount importance. I will do just about anything to get that first one out of the way. Once you have had sex one time, the flood gates will open. There will no longer be any awkward or uncomfortable situations because you have already been naked and intimate with each other. The whole relationship is easier once you get the first bang session out of the way! You can stop worrying if your place is dirty when she comes over. You can stop worrying if you smell good or not. You can take her to cheaper restaurants. You can grab her ass whenever you want. You can show up late. You can drunk-dial her. You don't have to shave before you see her. The list goes on and on. This is why it is important to sacrifice *everything* to sleep with her the first time.

Let's say all of your buddies are going to a big party. You want to go too, but this girl your dating wants to 'hang out' that night. Well, you have to hang out with her and miss that great party. That might be the night you close the deal! If you had already closed the deal, you could reschedule with her and go party with your bros.

Let's say she wants to go see some lame opera or play; you have to go and you have to pretend to like it. This is because you haven't banged her yet. After you have had sex you can simply tell her you'd rather go see the new Quentin Tarantino movie or watch the ballgame or something.

Let's say you are partying like a rock star at some night-club. You are dancing with some hot chick and having a great time. You get a text message from this other chick. She is drunk and she wants to see you. You've been out with her, but you haven't banged her yet. Well, unfortunately, you have to leave that great time and go see this girl and try to close the deal. Do whatever it takes to close the deal, and worry about everything else later.

## 47. Horned Up and Desperate

It really is okay to get horned up and desperate some-times. It's okay to put the beer-goggles on. It's okay to hook up with a fat chick once in a while. I have much more respect for a man that 'goes ugly' on occasion rather than some guy who gets laid twice a year and has no drive and no spirit. Men get urges bro! Sometimes you gotta take down a slumpbuster just to satisfy those urges. Never be ashamed to hook up with a less-than-attractive girl.

A good example of this occurred when we were at a beach volleyball tournament south of the San Diego border in Mexico. The Estero Beach Volleyball Tournament. This 'tournament' isn't really a tournament, it's more like a huge party on the beach where a handful of people play drunk volleyball. It's one hell of a good time. We hit it up every few years.

At this venue there is a main outside bar on the beach where everyone ends up partying. On this particular trip we all got drunk at the bar the first night. We reminisced about past stories since we hadn't seen each other for a while. It was great hanging out with the guys. We were drinking Dos Equis and doing tequila shots and getting rowdy. Partying Mexico style.

As the night went on, we couldn't avoid all these hot little chicks running around partying and dancing drunk. Our attention turned to chasing tail for the remainder of the night.

Eventually, we headed back to our tents. There are few hotel options available so just about everyone stays and camps in tents. There were so many tents it was literally called 'tent city.' Party Scars and Riki came back very late from the bar that night, after everyone else in tent city was asleep. I was already in my tent with a chick, naturally.

Scars saw me with a chick in my tent and he could tell I just got laid. He was very drunk, and very horny. And he hates it when I get laid and he doesn't. So now he really wanted to get some action for himself.

Party Scars is a buddy from Orange County. He is a legendary babe hound. He can hold his own against the best. He is tall, dark hair, good looking, and not shy. He and I are always jockeying to see who can score first. If we both hook up and one guy has a hotter chick, the other guy will dump his chick and attempt to trade-up.

Party Scars' problem is that he parties hard. And he thinks with his penis. Not a good combination. He earned his nickname from having new wounds every few months, all caused by partying mistakes. One time he started getting naked in Las Vegas casino at 5am in the morning. Riki and I were like 'What the fuck?!' His pants and underwear were at his ankles. We dragged him by his feet across the floor 40 yards into the elevator so he wouldn't get busted or thrown in jail. That gave him a horrible rug burn on his ass cheeks. He couldn't sit down for six weeks.

The worst one though occurred in Laughlin, Nevada on a Spring Break trip to Lake Havasu. Two white trash Laughlin local chicks were walking down the street drunk late at night. Scars was loaded too. He is aggressive with chicks and it usually gets good results. He can always fall back on his handsome face if things go wrong. This time however, he grabbed the wrong girl. This white trash broad had a nice body, great ass, and a big gap between her two front teeth. When he grabbed this chick's arm, she turned and cracked him in the face with a beer bottle. Straight away! It shattered the bottle and knocked him out cold. When he came to, nobody was around. He had a large gash on his face above his cheekbone near his eye. It was a bad cut. A couple weeks later he went to a beach party. While playing flippy-cup that day he was getting rowdy and fell down and got another cut on his other cheek. Instead of taking it easy and staying out of the sun, Scars got totally drunk and totally sunburn. The first big gash on his face got sunburn, leaving a permanent mark. Party Scars nickname was born.

Back to Mexico and the tents. It was late and Scars and Riki wanted some pussy. Riki knew his best option for getting laid was to fire up Scars. Riki encouraged Scars to go tent-to-tent looking for a chick to hook up with. He said, "Scars, remember all those girls we saw out tonight? You know some of them must want to get laid!" Scars listened. Riki was a great motivator, and Scars was very gullible, and very horny.

So drunk-ass Scars starts going into *every* random tent. People were like, "What the fuck?!" I poked my head out of my tent and couldn't believe what Scars was doing. I thought somebody was going to kick his ass for sure. He was unzipping random tents, popping in, getting kicked out of tents, girls were shrieking, guys were saying, "Get the fuck out of here!" and yet Riki was still saying, "Scars, try this tent, Scars, try that tent…"

A couple guys got really pissed. Scars just said, "Policia, policia, no problema."

Then, to my amazement, only about the seventh or eighth tent he went into, he didn't come out of for 10 or 15 minutes.

He finally came crawling out. And he had chick in tow. He was pulling some chick out with him! Brought her out and right into his tent! I was shocked.

I guess this girl's friend had some guy in their tent and they were getting it on. They wanted some privacy. Scars had come along at the perfect time.

In no time at all we could hear Scars getting laid. Riki and I kept peeking in. His feet were sticking out the tent. We were tickling his feet and trying to mess up his bang session. One of them threw a shoe and hit me in the head, then they zipped up the tent.

The next day Scars had a terrible hangover. All of us were eating breakfast at the cantina on the beach. We kept asking him about last night. Pulling a chick that late under those circumstances was pretty damn impressive. Scars was hungover and reluctant to talk about it. We weren't going to let him shrug this one off; we insisted on hearing everything. He finally gave in and started telling us how he got her out of that tent and what he said, shit like that. We wanted all details. Scars seemed queasy, but finally he told us about banging her. He said his only intention was trying to score and he was hammered so he hadn't really got a good look at the chick. Not until he started boning her. I remember him showing us how he was leaning up with his arms fully extended while he was pumping her in the missionary position. He said he was up like that so he could see her boobs and her face. He said he had to squeeze his eyes shut and then open them a couple times just to focus because it was dark and he was drunk. He was explaining how he was trying to focus so he could see what she looked like. He said when he finally focused on her face, he noticed how disgustingly ugly she was and he gagged immediately. He made a gagging motion.

By all accounts, she was extremely fugly. He said she had teeth like those fake teeth you see people wearing on Halloween. She had a greasy, crooked face with multiple pimples. She had bruises all over her body. She was slightly chubby with stretch marks on her boobs. Scars said he was repulsed. (He was so serious in the way he told us that we couldn't help but laugh) He said that after he gagged he continued boning her but with his head turned all the way to the side, looking away at the side of the tent. He showed us his pumping motion and how he had his head turned to the side. I spit my breakfast out with laughter. All of us were laughing uncontrollably. Scars was not laughing; he was repulsed thinking about it. He kind of shuddered and shook his head thinking about it.

I've never been with a chick so ugly I couldn't look at her. At least Scars finished the job. Riki and I were proud of him. Some guys get desperate and there is nothing wrong with that.

A little addition to that story occurred later at breakfast. We were about to leave when Scars said in a low voice, "Holy crap there she is." The five of us at the table looked, and Ooo-fah! There she was. She was a solid 2. Scars described her perfectly. She was extremely fugly.

I thought it would be funny if I called her over and embarrassed Scars. I love doing that. So I said, "Yolonda! Heyyyy Yolandaaa." Well this dumb broad with jacked up teeth and a crooked face and a couple fat rolls comes over to our table all smiling and sits on *my* lap and starts rubbing her fingers through *my* hair. She didn't even look at Scars. She thought I was the one from last night! My joke had backfired. Those guys, especially Scars, thought it was hilarious. I tried to explain to her that Scars was the one she liked but she kept petting me. Those guys kept saying how I really like her and she believed them. They were really enjoying the mix-up at my expense. Yolanda finally left. She winked at me on the way out. End of that story.

## 48. Women love a challenge

When it comes to men, women love a challenge. Women want to win a guy over. They want a guy who keeps them guessing. They want a man who is difficult to figure out. Surely, they don't want some sappy, kiss-ass guy who is at their beckoning call anytime they wish. The problem is, how do you become this elusive, sought-after guy, when you are actually pursuing her and trying to win her over? That is a question for the ages.

Basically, you have to have the right mix of showing her you are interested, yet not being whipped over her. You need to call her at the right times. And you need to *not* call her occasionally when she is expecting your call. You need to talk to her and make her feel wanted. But you also need to look away and stare into space so she has to look at you and wonder if you are sincere or not. You need to show up and surprise her sometimes, yet you also need to be a little flaky. You need to make some time for her and give her some attention, but she also needs to see that you are a busy person and you have a lot shit going on. Women love a guy with a lot on his plate. A busy guy with many things going on in his life is desirable. Women are attracted to this because they feel honored that you are fitting her into your schedule. They like winning you over and *earning* more of your time.

I was kind of dating this really hot pharmaceutical sales chick last year. I knew she thought she was hot shit because she had a small tight ass, good size boobs, and a hot face. She looked like the lead singer from Pussycat Dolls; not that hot, but close. I needed to somehow put this chick in her place and become a challenge to her.

I began by only talking to her once a week. She would ask me what was going on and I would tell her I was really busy at work; I had poker night on Monday's, basketball on Wednesdays, a late meeting on Thursday, Friday I needed to hang out with my buddies, and on the weekend I was working on this new internet project. I wasn't really *that* busy, but I wanted to make her understand that she wasn't the most important thing in the world to me. I'm sure she was accustomed to guys dropping everything to spend time with her. She asked me if I wanted to go to some concert in the park on Saturday. I said that I'd love to but I needed to concentrate on getting this new internet project off the ground. I went into detail and told her how important it was. She understood. I *did not* reschedule something with her. I told her, "Okay, I'll talk to you soon." I didn't say, "Sorry I can't, how about tomorrow or the next day?" Hell no. That is too sappy and she would still think she had me eating out of her hand. By saying, 'Talk to you soon,' it left it up in the air when we would talk again. Thus, when I did call her a few days later, I could tell she was pleasantly surprised to hear from me. I then said "How you been? I have tickets to the game on Thursday, You wanna go?" Affirmative. She warmed up to me from that point on and she was always requesting time with me. I sealed the deal that weekend.

# III. Post-Bang

## 49. A Rotation

Baseball teams need a good starting rotation to get them to the playoffs. I need a good rotation of women in my life to keep it exciting.

Make the most of your life as a single man and date multiple women. When you decide to settle down and get married you'll be stuck with one woman for your entire life. You'll have plenty of time to be with one woman then. Until then, if you are not in a serious relationship, work on getting a rotation of women you can see on a regular basis. Dating different women can be dynamic and adventurous. You will find that you enjoy certain qualities of each and every woman in your rotation.

Maybe one girl you are dating loves sports and she can hang out and watch a ballgame anytime. Maybe one girl you are dating is totally intellectual. You like just hanging out with her and talking or going to a museum. Maybe one chick you are dating is a nympho and loves having sex 24/7. Maybe one girl you are dating is really young and innocent and she lives in a sorority and you like hearing about her college lifestyle. Maybe one chick you are dating is romantic and loves having candlelight dinners. Or maybe one chick you are dating is this hot brunette who has the best real D-cup boobs you have ever seen with dark brown Italian silver dollar nipples and she rarely wears a bra and you can't stop thinking about them. Ugghh! I miss that chick! Anyway, I could go on and on. Dating multiple women is an experience all men should consider. There are too many things about too many women I want to discover.

It is not easily juggling women. It's tedious work constantly trying to figure out who to go out with, which phone call you should answer, which call you should let go to voicemail, when to have sex with each one so you keep her happy, when to drunk-dial them, etc.

I have become excellent at managing a rotation. My buddy Derek is the best at it though, and Party Scars is the worst at it.

Scars will be juggling five chicks at one time. He always has the worst rotation. Two will be smoking hot bleach-blond sexy club-hopping chicks who can't do basic arithmetic. Another one will be a brunette psycho chick who he will eventually have to get a restraining order against. Throw in a butt-ugly Asian with big, fake, circus boobs and a blond hillbilly milf. That's Scars's rotation.

We'll run into one of the hot blonds at a nightclub and she'll be dressed in a short, tight skirt, lots of cleavage, lots of hairspray. Every guy in the place will be salivating over this girl, but she will be all over Scars. Then he will leave, without her, and go see one of the ugly chicks he is dating. Huh?! Yeah, I don't get it. And the more Scars dogs her, the more she likes him. They'll be blowing up his cell phone all night long.

Scars will do stupid things like one time he left a used condom on top of his waste basket by his desk. The hottest chick in his rotation found it. She went ballistic. Scars showed up to a party with a black eye one time and told us all about it. Scars is just terrible at managing his rotation. Sometimes two chicks will show up at the same time late night at his house. Sometimes Scars will show up to a wedding or event with his 5th starter or middle reliever, the worst chick in his rotation. Crap like that. When I go to a wedding, I bring the best girl in my rotation so I can show off a little bit, right?!

A friend of mine, Derek, is an expert at juggling a rotation. He has a system for building a solid rotation. If he is in a dry spell, he will start juggling a bunch of slumpbusters. He'll just start dating ugly chicks. He doesn't care. It makes him happy because at least he is getting some late night lovin. Then he will find a 5 or 6 who is into him (a 5 or 6 on a scale of 1-10, 10 being a goddess.) Derek will then let go of his worst slumpbuster to make room for this newfound 6. Once he has all 6s in his rotation, he will start shooting for 7s and 8s. If he finds one worth dating, the worst girl in his rotation gets booted out. He is constantly upgrading his harem. He works this all the way up until his is dating a couple 7s, a couple 8s, and a 9. Derek has some serious game too. He lives in NYC and every time I see him he has 9s hanging on him and he is still trying to work on some other 9 or 10. Now that is how you manage a starting rotation!

The last bit of advice I can give about procuring a rotation is that every once in a while, you need to dump your entire rotation. Last New Years I had all kinds of crap going on in my life and I was getting bogged down by my rotation. They were all wanting to spend more time with me. They were all nagging me. I needed some space man. I stopped returning all phone calls and told them all I needed some freedom. See ya. Kissing my whole rotation goodbye helped me concentrate on my job and all of the other things in my life. I worked everything out and felt much better. I then began working on a new rotation. And starting a new rotation is always fresh and exhilarating.

## 50. Pimpin Ain't Easy

Maintaining a rotation is much more difficult than it may seem (but still fun of course.) Dating multiple women can become a chore. The first problem is that all these women will be demanding more of your free time. Outside of your job, you only have so much time during the week to hang out with a girl. The more women you are dating, the less free time you will have, and that will get on your nerves.

Keeping up with the different things going on in each girl's life can be a tall order. I will be out with Rachel and ask her how her cat is doing. She will say, "I don't have a cat!" I will be out with Kelly and tell her how I won the poker tournament I played in last week. She will tell me as she rolls her eyes, "You already told me that." It gets worse too. One girl will call me and I'll be drunk and I'll say, "How was your work party babe?!" She'll yell, "I didn't have a work party! What are you talking about!?" That's when they start to get suspicious and problems arise.

Another obstacle is scheduling time with your girls. One girl always has some special occasion you need to attend. One girl wants to see you at least once a week, so you have to schedule time to see her. One girl will be on the rag that weekend and you'll be like, "Why am I wasting my damn time over here?! I should be at my other hos house."

Scheduling all these dates requires a lot of effort. The worst is when I go away for a weekend with the boys. If I am leaving on a Friday, I have to service Rachel on Tuesday, Kelly on Wednesday, and Monique on Thursday just to keep them happy. Otherwise they will be cockstarved while I am gone and I don't want some other dude servicing them. By the time I go on vacation I am exhausted.

Other problems arise from dating multiple women. Here are some expert tips for your rotation.

~ Cell phones. They can get you in a lot of trouble. I know a number of couples that have broken up over cell phone bills. They are hard evidence of who you were calling and what time you made that call. Be careful bro!

Some girls like to go through your phone to see who you have called or text messaged. Putting your phone on lock mode will only make you look suspicious. Instead, I give all my side chicks guy's names. Let's say my main girl's name is Monique, and I know she is the type who will search through my phone if I am at her place passed out drunk after sex. I will have Kelly's name in there as Kevin K., and Rachel's name in there as Richard. Then I'm in the clear for any phone call or text message.

~ Perfume. Another wise move is to buy all your chicks the same perfume. Who cares what it smells like. The point here is to avoid having your sheets or clothing or your body smelling like some other chick's perfume. If they all have the same perfume, you are golden and have nothing to worry about.

~ Sheets. Keep them clean. Don't let last night's stain ruin tonight's game.

~ Pop-ins. Do not allow at pop-ins. Draw the line. Let them know that they are *not* allowed to show up to your home unannounced. Get really pissed and tell them that how rude that is and that they need to have more respect for you. Pop-ins will get you busted for sure, so put your foot down and disallow them.

As Justin Timberlake once said on the Tonight Show, "Pimpin ain't easy, but it sho is fun!"

## 51.  Packs Of Hounds

Let me tell ya, if you are letting your girl hang around a bunch of horny guys, you are just asking for trouble. If she's a girl you just met, and you can tell she digs you, it's wise try and get her out of the nightclub, or at least over to your table. This will prevent her from losing interest in you and finding another guy. A change of venue is stimulating, and you might even get her to come home with you. Furthermore, a change of venue is somewhat like a first date. She will be more comfortable with you the next time she sees you.

Leaving your girl alone just for a minute in a bar is risky. I've seen many guys return from the bathroom to find their target talking to another guy. This has happened to the best of us, so you just have to keep her attention on you, and keep trying to get her home. This also goes for hanging out at an afterparty, or even back at your own party. I have had roommates try to steal my chick before because they knew I had just met her. But I've been guilty of that too.

Outside of this nightclub we were preparing to head home recently. It was 2am. Erik noticed two chicks outside of the club. They looked ready to party. They were from Vegas, in town for the weekend. California bars close at 2am so they probably were not used to going home this early. The five of us corralled them and talked them into coming back to Erik's house for an afterparty. My buddy Mark immediately dove on the uber ugly one, which left the hot Asian one as open game. It was between me, my Italian buddy Salami, Riki and Erik. Salami was tired and sleepy. Riki and I tried, but Erik was clearly in. They were kissing and she had her hands on his lap. We drove back to Erik's house. At the house I threw on some Tupac, low volume, and Riki turned on the porn channel. Erik went to the bathroom.

Hot Vegas Asian girl sits on the couch. She had a solid body, C-cups, lots of makeup and an overall promiscuous look to her. Great piece of ass for such a late night pull. I couldn't resist. I was grabbing her trying to make out with her. We almost kissed, but she was hesitant. Boy I could tell she was horny. She liked the porno, and she liked it when I whipped out my cock. Yeah, I whipped it out. I got a good read on her - I knew she wanted cock. She wasn't shocked at all when I pulled it out. I thought it was on, but I think she liked Erik better. Erik came out of the bathroom. He gave me a dirty look. He manned-up and grabbed her by the hand and took her back to his room. Oh well.

Erik was in there fooling around with her for ten or fifteen minutes.

Then somehow Erik's TV got all messed up and none of the channels would work. Only Erik knew how to fix his many components. Riki yelled, "The TV won't work."

If it were me, I would let them figure out how to fix the TV, or I would fix it in the morning. But Erik is the type of guy where if something isn't working he has to fix it right then and there. He is just that type of person.

Erik came out of his room frustrated. He looks at the blank TV and began to fiddle with all the components. I decided to slip into his room while he was working on the TV.

It was pitch black dark when I got in there. Soon I hear, "Do you want me to suck it now?" Erik must have gotten her all warmed up. She was ready to give him a blowjob now.

I quietly pulled the handle down on the door and gently closed it shut. I instantly got buck naked and crawled in bed to see what would happen. I still hadn't answered her question. I couldn't answer because she would hear that my voice was different from Erik's. She reached over and touched me. So I just got up there and straddled her chest, putting my cock right in front of her face. She took my cock and stuffed it down her throat. I was like WOW! I had my hands and forearms pressed up against the wall above the headboard. She was doing all the work and giving me one great hummer. She pulled it out and in her sexy Asian voice said, "Cum on my tits Ok," and then stuffed my cock back in her mouth. I thought, 'This girl is a champion!' I answered her, "Mmhmm," in a deep voice like Erik's. This chick was doing such a good job that I blew it all over her in about 5 minutes. It was awesome!!! It was simply one heck of a super blowjob.

Then I was like, 'Shit what do I do now?' She asked me some question, but I couldn't answer. I still couldn't speak or she would recognize my voice. I handed her a small towel, gathered my clothes and walked out. I made it to the bathroom across the hall, narrowly missing Erik as he walked back into his room. He had fixed the TV and was now ready to get down to business with his girl.

He told us this later: He closed the door and was starting to take his clothes off in the dark. As he was taking his boxers off, Vegas Asian said, "Thank you for cumming all over me. I liked that!"

Erik froze for a second. He tried to understand the words that had just been spoken. I can just imagine him putting two and two together and figuring out what had just happened. I still crack up thinking about his reaction. He figured it out. He mumbled, "Dammit Billy," under his breath. He let out a big sigh. Then he climbed in bed with her.

He ended up pummeling her a couple times that night and still had a good time. Erik was a good sport about it. Mark pummeled her ugly friend in the garage. Riki watched some porn and then went home. I passed out on the couch.

## 52. The Secret To Getting Bootie Calls

Do you want to have 5 or 6 chicks in your cell phone that you can call late night, any night, and get some ass? Do you want chicks that you have hooked up with previously to call you randomly on weekend nights looking to get laid? Ever had a night where you strikeout at the bars, its 2am, and you are dying for some pussy, any pussy?

Well here is the secret to getting bootie calls. And it is not really a secret so don't expect an earth-shattering, totally enlightening piece of advice here. Here it is: You have to lick the pink taco. You have to lick her snatch like you are in the state finals of pie-eating contest. You have to do it the very first time you have the opportunity, and you have to do it well. You need to go downtown and not come back up until she has been completely satisfied. Furthermore, you have to act like that's all you want to do Son - like you are perfectly happy munching box and you *don't even care* about getting laid. That's what you gotta do.

Of course, banging after you're done is a given. You are a man right! But tomorrow, she won't remember the banging. All she is going to be thinking about is how you went down on her and how good it made her feel. You can bet the next time she is drunk and horny she'll be blowing up your cell phone fo sho!

From then on, anytime you want to tap that ass, just call her up and she'll invite you over without hesitation.

Now, truth be told, I am not an expert at this like I would like to be. I have seen others reap the benefits of being an expert in this field, so I am learning. My buddy Gooch is the virtuoso of box lickers. You should see that dude's cell phone light up like a Christmas tree every night we are out. Girls will be texting dirty messages, calling him five times in a row, all kinds of shit. I know that if we haven't hooked up by 2am, I am on my own because Gooch will slip out of the club to go pummel some chick. Next day he is telling me all about him banging some bootie call (I demand all banging details from all my friends.) Every story he tells has a ½ hour pussylicking part to it. Finally, it dawned on me, "Damn I need to start licking more box..." I did, and sure enough, I got chicks calling me late night. So now you know the secret to getting bootie calls. Just go downtown brutha.

## 53. Service Chicks Immediately After Vacations

I recently had this quandary. This chick I met a few weeks ago is getting back from South Beach tonight and she wants to see me. However, there is a big poker game I was invited to and I love no limit Texas Hold'em. What do I do?

Here is what I based my decision on. Normally I would head to the poker game because I can always tap that ass later. However, there were two important factors at play here. One is that I haven't tapped that ass yet, and I really want to. We've only been dating a few weeks. After you have sex with a chick once, it makes it a thousand times easier to have sex with her again. The first time is always the toughest, obviously.

The second reason I balked at playing cards is that she had just spent four days in Miami on business. She was probably tan, hot, and horny from laying out at the beach and seeing all that skin in Miami. When chicks get back from vacation they are still in a vacation mood and need to be serviced asap. (If they're not horny and don't need to be serviced asap, they probably got boned while on vacation and that's all bad.)

Anyway, if I waited a couple days like I normally would, she would have settled back into her day to day routine. She'd be back in her home city, working her 9 to 5 job; she'd lose the vacation mood she was in and all the horniness that comes with it. It would be much more difficult to get laid with this chick. I'd have to go out to dinners with her, buy her flowers, act real nice around her, etc. I knew I needed to go see her right away. Sure enough, she was craving for a good bang session. It was great. Even better, I got the first one out of the way too so the floodgates opened and I banged her all week.

## 54. Drunk-Dials

Don't believe the misperception that late night drunk-dials are a bad thing. True that many drunk-dials are regrettable, but many work out better than you expect.

Calling a girl when you are shitfaced drunk will definitely annoy her. But the next morning she will remember your call, and she'll be glad you thought about her. It's a sign that you really like her. This is fine of you do like the girl.

Drunk-dials tell a girl that you are thinking about her when you are at you worst. This is somewhat flattering to a girl. It is an indirect way of letting a girl know she is special. It also lets her know that you are not out with another woman late night. Add all these up and you come to realize that the occasional drunk-dial is a good idea.

Problem is, guys will drunk-dial chicks they like, chicks they don't like, chicks they just want to bone, chicks they just met, chicks they've broken up with, chicks they think are ugly when they are sober, and any other chick who's number is in their phone. These drunk-dials turn into attempted bootie calls and they rarely work out. That's why most drunk-dials are regrettable. Only call chicks in your rotation late night.

If the situation is right, I will call *all* the girls in my rotation late night. One of them will want some late night lovin. The others will be pissed that I woke them up, but I will still score points with them because I called, and that will set up future bang sessions. Never underestimate the power a good drunk-dial.

## 55. Remain Friends With Hot Chicks

Stay friends with hot girls. Keep in touch with them. This may seem obvious, but I have seen many horny cavemen get pissed because hot chicks won't show them any love. They get so frustrated that they throw in the towel and lose contact with these hot chicks.

Staying friends with hotties could pay off bigtime down the road. Everyone knows some smoking hot chick that has given him the Heisman and denied all his advances. She might be a chick you liked, or maybe you dated; maybe she's a friend of a friend, or maybe you just got her phone number one random night and nothing ever materialized. Either way, you tried to score with her and things didn't work out. No need to sweat it. Just keep it cool with her. Remain in touch.

The really over-the-top hot girls deny guys all the time. This is normal. When this happens, most guys give up and move on. Some guys are suckers and they get classified as the girl's 'friend.' The girl tells her girlfriends, 'He is like a brother to me.' Some guys don't give up. They keep trying. They keep calling. They keep annoying the poor girl. Girls begins to think this guy is weird, or strange, or a psycho.

Do none of those things. If a chick is ridiculously hot and she has denied your advances, never sell out. Give her some distance. Don't talk to her for a week, or a few weeks. If you see her out at a bar nightclub, give her the cold shoulder - but in a nice way. Say she runs into you at a bar, she will expect a big hello from you. She'll expect you to be all over her and give her lots of attention. Instead, say to her, "Hey Megan!" and then immediately move on to something else. Pretend you were distracted. Leave her wanting more. She will be surprised, and she will subconsciously want to win you over again. She will wonder why you are giving her the cold shoulder. She needs to know that it is *not* Okay for her to cocktease you like she does with so many other guys. She needs to know you are different. After a week or two has gone by, give her a call or send her a text message. Text her, "Megs! We are at Such&Such bar, you should come meet up. Get yer ass over here! : )" That text message works often.

Many, many times I have stayed in contact with chicks that have initially rejected me. Often times I'll be rewarded for my patience. Sometimes I hang out with a hot chick for a while and they think all I want to do is bang them. (Where would they get that idea?) They flatly refuse my advances. Sometimes a hot girl I am chasing gets into a relationship with another guy. Sometimes a girl will think I am just not her 'type.' Regardless of the reason for the rejection, I hang around and keep in touch with these hot chicks. I stay friends with them. I text them once in a while. I might Myspace them a message. I might call them or invite them to a party. Sure enough, every so often, a hot piece of ass will fall in my lap! Girls go through phases where they need cock: breakups, horny spells, all kinds of shit. If you are the cool, down-to-earth, familiar guy waiting on the sidelines, you can service them when the time is right.

You know what else goes a long way? Send them a text or email on a holiday or their birthday. You get big points for that. On fun holidays like St Patrick's Day or Cinco De Mayo I will send one text message and address it to all the chicks in my phone. "Happy Cinco De Mayo!" It's surprising how many texts I'll get back from chicks I haven't heard from in a while.

Another way to stay in touch with hotties: randomly ask them out for tea or coffee. Most guys don't do that kind of stuff with chicks who have rejected them. They will appreciate your offer. It will seem like a sincere gesture to remain friends. You never know where it will lead.

Sometimes I will send a text message to a girl that I haven't talked to in a few weeks telling her that, 'We are all going out dancing, wish you were here!' That will get her attention, and often times she will want to meet up and have some fun.

I've got many examples of how this perseverance has paid off. Here is one.

I knew this really sexy, smoking hot, blond bartender named Sheri. She had an ass you could eat off of. It was perfect! She was a petite girl with nice, natural, ski-jumper boobs, and just a gorgeous face. So just about the time I had her all ready to go out with me, she developed a serious boyfriend.

Dammit! They went out and got even more serious, and even moved in with each other. I was pissed.

All her other guy-friends dropped off. I kept in contact with her. Sent her an occasional Myspace message. We exchanged texts once in a while. I would go see her at the bar she was working at occasionally. I would go out to lunch with her every couple months. Every time I would see her I would say this, "Are you still dating *that* guy?" I knew they were still together, but wanted to let her know I was curious. That question, and the way I phrased it, was kind of a backdoor way of letting her know that I was still interested. It also lets her know I am being nice about it and not telling her, "Dump that loser and go out with me." I was not overstepping my boundaries or blowing my nice guy image, but I was letting her know that I was still there waiting on the sidelines.

I got drunk at her bar one night and told her, "Sheri, have you ever been to a deli where they make you pull out one of those tickets and that's your number in line?" She nodded yes. I continued, "Well, I have ticket number one if you and Whats-his-face ever break up." She smiled and went back to pouring drinks.

Eventually Sheri and her boyfriend broke up. Guess who the rebound guy was? It worked out quite well. Quite quite well!

One time I remained friends with this swimsuit model, Stephanie, for over a year. She was so fricken hot - I can't explain how hot and sexy and cute and beautiful this chick was. Dark hair, blue eyes, perfect fricken body. I am a sucker for firm natural boobs, and she had em. I went out with her on a couple dates, everything went great; then she put the brakes on and we drifted apart. I think she somehow got the idea that I dated a lot of women, and she didn't like that. She still lived with her parents and I owned a condo not far away. She liked to yap on the phone all the time, so we still kept in touch. Went out to lunch a couple times, etc. She got a boyfriend so we kept in touch less often. Then she dumped the boyfriend and I thought I had a chance, but still nothing happened. I was pissed and really wanted to blow her off. I was very frustrated because I really thought this chick was the cat's meow.

After what seemed like an eternity, 10 or 12 months, we ended up at my house drinking wine one night. I still didn't think anything would happen because she had thwarted so many of my advances. Next thing I know we are in my bed getting naked. I was thrilled, but I *still* wasn't sure if she was going to let me close the deal. Was I about to bone this chick who I had salivated over for more than a year? Her body was a solid 10. I was incredibly turned on. I'll never forget what she said to me when we were under the sheets, "Don't cum too quickly, I want this to last."

"Oh my God, I am actually going to do this! Yes yes yes!" That's what went through my head. I realized I was about to get laid, and with one of the hottest chicks I had ever met! That in itself was a huge moment of exuberance.

I slid it in real slow.....got all the way in....and then had to slide it right back out. I was overcome with excitement. No sooner did I slip it in than I was ready to blow my load. Ooofah! I arched my ass up in the air so my dick pointed down and I blew a big load all over my sheets. "Oh geez, Oh No!!!!! What have I done?"

Talk about Two-Pump Chump; I was a *one pump* chump.

I had just done exactly what she told me not to do. I was really embarrassed. I hoped she wasn't aware of what had just happened. I tried to regain my composure. I was breathing heavily, so this was hard to do. I kissed on her neck to distract her. I then wiped myself off on the sheets a little bit and went back inside her. Fortunately, I was really into this chick and I was able to regain full hardness and keep the party going. I thought I redeemed my actions by having some really good sex with her for a good amount of time. I pulled out and had an incredible orgasm (one that I didn't have to conceal). She seemed like she really enjoyed it too.

As she walked to the bathroom she said, "Wow that was pretty good; I can't believe you came twice."

I winced with embarrassment.

She spent the night and we had some even better sex in the morning. That girl Stephanie was one I will never forget. Having sex with her was one of my greatest accomplishments as a man. But boy, what a poor performance I originally gave. We dated a few weeks and then she broke it off. I was bummed about that, but those memories of her are priceless. Always keep in touch with super-hot women.

## 56.  Unreliable Dog

Chicks that have guys at their beckoning call will soon lose interest in that guy. Don't be one of those guys. Don't be the guy who calls a girl on the phone all the time. Don't be a guy who wants a date every Friday night like clockwork. Don't be a guy who is predictable.

Be unpredictable. Be a little unreliable. Dog her once in a while. As I have said, keep her guessing. This will allow you to call her unexpectedly. This will allow you to pleasantly surprise her. You want her thinking, "I can't figure this guy out.' You'll have plenty of time to be the nice, reliable guy once you two have been with each other for months and months and have become boyfriend/girlfriend. But to win her initial attraction you have to be a dog.

Never call a girl more often than she calls you. I have a buddy who will call or text a new chick he has met 3 or 4 times in the first week. They will talk often, but she will never call him. That is such a turn-off! You might become friends with her, but there is *no way* you will ever get in her pants. No girl in the world will say to herself, "I like this guy because he calls me all the time and wants to see me all time." You win a girl over by actions and words, by charm and wit, not by being reliable.

Dog chicks and resist urges to smother them with attention. Fight the urges you have to call her all the time! This is difficult because she is hot and you will be thinking about her all the time. Every other guy does that - you have to be different. **To get women you normally wouldn't get, you have to do things you normally wouldn't do.** This includes *not* clearing up your entire weekend to spend time with her. This includes *not* taking her to the fanciest restaurant in town. This includes *not* texting her back immediately after she texts you (give it 20 minutes or an hour, etc). This includes *not* being the one to send the last text message during every text conversation.

If you want to get her attention, send her flowers on a random day with just a note saying "Thinking about you." That works for me. But the flowers will only be effective if you haven't talked to her in a while. If you talked to her yesterday, and then send her flowers, it won't be a big deal. If you dogged her for five days and then send her those flowers, her panties will start tingling.

The problem with meeting a chick you are really attracted to is that your first impulse is to treat her like a queen. Bad move. Ever notice how you treat chicks with whom you are mildly interested in? Ever notice how you treat the chicks you just want to sleep with? You are not the stand-up guy, perfect gentlemen-type with them, are you? You are a dog.

You are not the perfect gentleman towards mediocre chicks, are you? With mediocre chicks, you act like hanging out with them is no big deal. You might treat them with disdain. You might act arrogant. This turns them on and always seems to get the chicks you aren't really interested in whipped all over you.

The same is true for the girls you really like! You have to treat them the same way. Dog them occasionally. Be elusive. This will separate you from the pack. More times than not, she will want to win your attention.

## 57. Pussywhipped

It is a mistake to tell a girl, "I really like you" early in the dating process. It is a mistake to buy gifts for a girl too early on in a relationship. It is a mistake to call her your 'girlfriend' too soon. It is a mistake to spend all your time with a girl. It is a mistake to drop the L-bomb on a girl too soon. It is a mistake to ignore your buddies when you find a girl you like. It is a mistake to become submissive and let your girl make all the decisions. These are all examples of the genetic disorder called *Pussywhipped*. The ramifications of being pussywhipped can be very unhealthy.

Besides causing loss of mojo and masculinity, being pussywhipped can also cause you to lose the respect of your bros.

Never get whipped over some girl - she will consider it a major turn off. Women want a masculine guy. Women want a challenge. Women want a guy who can balance his friends and his job and his chick all at once. Throwing yourself at a girl is a sure-fire way to scare her off.

On the rare occasion that I meet a girl and start dating her and I actually do think she is pretty fricken special, I never tell her how I feel about her. Bite your tongue when those thoughts enter your mind! I know from experience that if I start throwing out the, "I really like you," it will affect the relationship in a negative manner. So I man-up and act like she is nothing special. This usually drives her crazy and makes her want me more.

I only tell a girl, "I really like you" when, in actuality, I don't really like her. I only say that to a girl if she is being a stubborn cocktease and I just want to score with her and not listen to her objections anymore. Then I know I will either score with her, or chase her away with my un-manly, "I really like you" confession.

## 58. Enjoy Dating

You will be tied down soon enough. Enjoy *not* being married. Enjoy dating. Dating beautiful women is one of the true luxuries of being an unmarried man. All your married buddies are jealous. Trust me.

There is no need to jump into a relationship and become boyfriend/girlfriend. If you are just 'dating,' you are provided with unlimited freedom. It's as close to having the best of both worlds as you can get. Too many sappy guys are anxious to start calling the girl they are dating their 'girlfriend.' That changes everything. Having a girlfriend is an extra level of commitment. When you are simply dating a girl you can hang out with the guys all the time. You can go out to bars and get drunk. You can chase women. You can bang random chicks and not feel guilty about it. You can go an entire night without calling your girl. You can go on weekend trips with the guys. All the while you can hang out with your girl whenever you want, bang her whenever you want, and feel completely free. When you have a girlfriend, the girl expects all that freedom to end. That means the party's over.

If you are young, and you are not dating as many women as possible, you are making a mistake. There are guys who date two or three chicks, then settle down and get married. Time goes by and they wonder what they missed. Those are the guys who end up disgruntled and eventually divorced. The guys who have experienced many women know a good one when they find one. Plus they have soiled their wild oats and are finally ready to settle down.

Enjoy the dating process. Don't be in a rush to jump from dating to a relationship. I remain 'dating' for as long as possible, even when I feel pressure from my girl to become boyfriend/girlfriend.

By the way, there is one defining way to recognize when a relationship has moved from dating to boyfriend/girlfriend status. When you are not worried about farting in front of your girl, that means you're in a relationship. Once you are comfortable ripping a fart in front of your chick, you have crossed the line. The party's over. You are no longer dating; you are committed and close to being in Lockdown. I'd much rather hold the fart in or excuse myself and go outside to rip a fart, rather than pass gas and be committed. Hold it in and make the dating process last as long as possible!

## 59. Sunday Nights Blow

Being married or having a steady girlfriend is great for Sunday nights. You can go rent a movie and snuggle on the couch, you can go see a movie, you can have dinner together, talk about your week, get laid; it's great. But the other 6 days a week - who needs em?! The only real time you crave having a steady girlfriend are Sunday nights. The only other time you crave a girlfriend is when you are going through times in your life.

Recognize this insecurity. Tell yourself the only reason I want a chick right now is because I lost my job, or because I haven't been laid in a while, or because my car broke down, or because the weather sucks, or because it's Sunday night, etc.

My pop once told me, "Every time tha man kicks you down, you gotta get right back up son." Don't wuss out and get a girlfriend because you are going through a rough patch in your life! Don't wuss out and desire a girlfriend so you can watch movies on Sunday nights. You will be miserable 6 days a week if you start a relationship with some chick just because you are lonely. Me, I get tired of most chicks after a couple weeks. Sometimes after a couple of hours. She has got to be pretty damn special for me to want to start a relationship with her. Yet time & again I see guys in relationships with chicks just because they need a companion around. Then they tell me, "Oh how wish I was single and banging chicks all time like you." Then a few years go by and they get divorced.

Coincidentally, the opposite holds true. When things aren't going good for ya, you want a girlfriend, but when things *are* going awesome for you, you want to be single and free and out on the town. That's why all these celebrities are always involved in break-ups. They are wealthy and successful and they want to be free. The goal is to find a happy medium. Don't get tied down with some broad when times are bad, and don't break up with a special chick when times are going good.

## 60. The Chase Is Half the Fun

Enjoy the *process* of meeting girls! The chase truly is half the fun. Being out on the town, running with friends, listening to music, getting drunk, chasing tail - that's what life's all about brutha. Don't get discouraged if you go out and you don't meet a girl. It happens to the best of us. Nobody I know scores all the time. Everyone has cold streaks. Nothin wrong with that. It should not be required that you need to meet a girl or get a phone number to have a good time! Laughing with buddies is part of a good night. Getting updates on what is going on in my friend's lives is part of a good night. Getting drunk is a good time. Seeing all the beautiful women is great. Watching buddies hook up with chicks is always entertaining. Watching buddies strikeout is always entertaining. Talking to a chick and not getting her number is always a learning experience. Just being able to be free and single is great. The chase is half the fun, so enjoy going out and partying!

## 61. Never Get Back With Your Ex

Let me give a statistic. 99% of couples who break up, then get back together again, do not stay together. The unfortunate truth is that they never make it. You have seen it hundreds of times: A guy and a girl break up, then they miss each other, so they get back together again. Well, the same issues are still there that broke them apart. Don't get back together again; it is a waste of time. It won't last. It will just cause more heartache on down the line. So just man-up and move on! Being single and free again is a good thing! Sitting around bummed out listening to Coldplay's *The Scientist* is not the answer. And getting back together with a woman just because you miss her is not the answer. There are plenty of other women out there! This is good wingman advice.

Now, that being said, you can definitely go back and have sex with your ex if you like. Nothin' wrong with sex with your ex. Just don't be a sucker and think the sex will make you two a good couple again.

## 62. Chicks Snoop

Chicks snoop through your shit man, so beware. Most girls I start dating eventually go through my shit in one way or another. I guarantee you will encounter a chick snooping through your stuff too. I don't know what they are looking for, but girls love to go through your belongings looking for incriminating stuff. Your girl is different though, she would never go through your shit, right? Wrong! Most girls do. Scratch that. All girls do.

Every girl that starts dating you develops an interest in you. Therefore, she wants to know what she is getting into. She wants to know if you have any skeletons in your closet. She wants to know what kind of guy you are. This is why chicks will snoop and go through your home like a private detective. They'll go through your dresser, your closet, your computer, your email, your jeans pockets, your receipts, your cell phone, your DVD collection looking for porn, your bathroom, your photographs, your mail, your credit card bills, your wallet, your couch cushions, your digital camera, and all kinds of other shit. Consider yourself warned.

I have seen many a good man go down ignoring this advice. My good buddy Carter told me his girlfriend never snooped. Then randomly he left his phone at her place. She decided to go through his text messages. Boom. Busted. See ya. His only defense was, "What the hell are you doing going through my shit?!" Well let me tell you friend; that dog don't bark. Forget about using that excuse as your only defense. She will walk out on you in a heartbeat if she finds something incriminating. Even if you stay together, the relationship won't be the same.

Its uncanny how many times I have said to myself, 'She won't look through that drawer,' or 'No way will she check my computer,' or 'No way will she realize there are new phone numbers in my phone.' In all instances she did, and I was busted. Guys could care less about that stuff. Chicks love to snoop. It's in their nature.

I thought I had learned my lesson and was cautious enough now. But of course, last night right after I finished banging this girl I am dating, I jumped in the shower. By the time I got out she had went through my computer, found this file, and read all my notes and ideas for this book. I threw out there the, "Why are you going through my shit goddamit?!" She didn't give a crap about that. I tried to counter with, "That's not mine; I'm just editing a book for a friend." She fired back, "Bullshit! I've heard you say 'Nice guys finish last!'" And what's this: 'Don't bring sand to the beach?!' Is that why you never take me out with your friends?!!"

I was busted and it was no fun at all. As a wingman, I implore you to keep your cell phone locked, your email confidential, your condoms hidden, and all your private stuff private.

## 63. Psycho Chicks

As you traverse through the myriad of women in your life, it is inevitable that you will run into a psycho chick or two. Run for the hills any time you find yourself involved with a psycho chick. This is your warning. Psycho chicks can really mess up your world. Compounding the problem is that psycho chicks are usually very good in bed. They can rock your world. They are so into you, and they have a strong desire to please you - this leads to *very* good sex. Ignore this. Run for the hills. Psycho women have no common sense and they can and will wreak havoc in your life.

Psycho chicks will do things that make no sense at all. This is no laughing matter. They may even evolve into a Level 3 Clingon or a stalker. A Level 3 Clingon is a chick who refuses to leave your side and attempts to put you in Snuggle Lockdown every night. A Level 3 Clingon's goal is to advance your relationship into boyfriend/girlfriend Lockdown status immediately.

A stalker is a psycho chick who follows you and refuses to leave you alone. Stalkers, psychos, and Level 3 Clingons should be renounced and avoided at all cost.

Everyone I know has some psycho-chick experience. The best way to warn others about these type of women are to offer a few real-life examples of psycho-chick stories that happened to friends of mine. Learn from these, and like I said, the first hint you get that your girl might be psycho, you need to run and hide and get out of that situation.

- My buddy Todd dated this chick for 6 months before he realized she was psycho. They got into some massive fights, most of them in public. She would scream at the top of her lungs at him no matter where they were.

*Point of Advice: One obvious sign a chick has psycho tendencies is her willingness to fight or scream in public.*

They broke up, but she would still come over to his house. The sex was hard to resist. Then they would get into fights and she would try to kick his ass. Todd finally had to go to court and get a restraining order against her. Then she went and got one against him. This affected all of us because Todd would always want us to go very early to the club. He would get there early, show the bar manager the restraining order, and then have dibs on the place all night. If she showed up, she would have to leave because he was their first. If she showed up first, we would all have to leave. So it became a contest on who would get to the latest hotspot first. It was a real pain in the ass.

- My first experience with a psycho chick was in college. I was banging this hot waitress who lived about 45 minutes away. She would come see me every weekend. I knew her for about a month when one day I was getting a Father's Day card ready to mail to my dad for Father's Day. She was there watching me lick the stamp and stuff like that. Then she said something I will never forget, "What if I gave you a Father's Day card?" I laughed for a second and said, "Yeah, right." Then I started to think about what she was implying. I was like, 'Holy shit, this chick is considering having my kid.'

I had only known her a month. Before her comment I had already detected some psycho tendencies. I thought she liked me a little too much for just knowing me for a month. Her comment/joke was the deciding factor. I realized she was more trouble than good. I stopped calling her or answering her calls. Sure enough, she was psycho. She came to my work and caused a big scene. She called me three of four times a day, every day. It was a mess. I considered myself lucky that I figured it out early.

*Point of Advice: Relationships that evolve too quickly usually go down in flames just as quickly. Females who try to push relationships immediately into boyfriend/girlfriend status, or marriage, kids, etc., are psychos. These relationships never last. Normal relationships gradually evolve and do not need to be rushed.*

- My buddy Davis was dating this girl when he was living in Colorado playing college baseball. The baseball program was cut at his school so he figured he'd move back to Cali. His chick didn't take the news too well. She made him a videotape of long songs and poetry and psycho crap like that and gave it to him and begged him to stay. Psycho!

He ended it though and moved to Cali. He cut off all contact with her. Three months went by. He had a new girlfriend and a new life. One night he got a phone call from her and he actually answered it this time. He wanted to tell her to stop calling him. She was crying on the phone and blabbering about wanting to see him. She was crying so much that Davis said, "Oh I'd like to see you too, but we need to move on." That's all she needed to hear. Five minutes later there was a knock at his door. Next thing he knew she was standing in his living room. Needless to say, he was very surprised. She told him how she had moved a few blocks away and lived very close to him! Psycho! He was freaked out. She went on to tell him how she was in love with him and missed him terribly and didn't want to be without him. He was really freaked out now. He wanted this chick out of his life for sure.

As soon as they were done having sex, Davis told her in no uncertain terms that she needed to stop contacting him. Yeah, that psycho sex is hard to turn down. His resolution to end it made her cry even more. He regretted banging her already. He literally had to shut the door on her and lock it. She was a psycho so the phone calls didn't stop. He would run into her at random places like the grocery store, baseball games, and parties. He said it took a year for that psycho chick to leave him alone and he still gets occasion phone calls from her.

- The last psycho story I will tell you is the worst one of them all. It's so bad, that if it wasn't a very good friend of mine, I wouldn't have believed it. He will remain nameless. He told me about it in confidence. Most of our other friends still don't know about this story.

My buddy started dating this really wild party-animal chick. She was a cougar with blond hair and huge fake mismatching tits. She was from South Beach Miami. She went to afterparties all the time, did drugs, etc. A girl you really want to bring home to mom. Ya right. None of us could figure out why he was dating this party tramp. My buddy was a stud. He made a lot of money, owned a phat townhouse, and got chicks all the time. Him and I ran together for a year straight in Chicago. We took down a lot of scores that year. My best guess was he just wanted to date a wild chick for once.

My buddy had never been in a threesome. He was a greenhorn when it came to wild stuff like that. I was from California, so I was the opposite. He knew my background and was probably looking to try some crazy stuff too. Miami Tramp would tell him how she had been in many threesomes, gangbangs, you name it. She would say to him "You've *got* to try a threesome. I can't believe you've never had one! I'll try to set one up." I thought she was just stringing him along. I met her a couple times and could tell she loved my buddy. My buddy was a dream for a girl like that.

A couple months went by. My buddy told me we need to go out to lunch so he can tell me about his weekend. We went out for lunch. He was beaming. He told me it finally happened. My buddy was no longer a threesome virgin! I wanted all the details.

He said his girl had a friend in town who was flight attendant from Atlanta. She flew into town and they all went out. At the end of the night they were all at his house. One thing leads to another and he starts banging the other girl on the chair in his bedroom. Nice! Miami Tramp walked in the room, was a little surprised, but okay with it. She was just watching and playing with his balls and stuff like that. He went into more details, and told me all about it.

I was proud of my bro. He had his first threesome!

Another month went by. He and I went to lunch again. This time he was not beaming, not at all.

My buddy always wears a condom, but not that night. He told me he wasn't prepared when the Atlanta chick jumped on him and the sex just started happening, right away, so he just went with it. He was boning the Atlanta girl and about to cum. Then, his girlfriend happened to jump on him at the wrong time. He wasn't able to pull out. He told me he has been a little worried about that for the past few weeks.

The Atlanta chick flew back home, and he hasn't heard from her, so he thought everything was fine. Then he got a phone call. The psycho flight attendant was pregnant and insisting on having the baby. Ooofah!

She was a 34 year-old psycho who just wanted a kid. My buddy was screwed. He did a lot of research and found out that this is a new, common occurrence. There are older women out there who are predatory and looking for guys with good genes to get impregnated by.

My buddy's girlfriend, Miami Tramp, must have been telling her flight attendant friend how great of a guy my buddy was. Atlanta Psycho probably planned the whole thing. Shit, Miami Tramp might have planned it from the getgo for all we know.

My buddy hired a lawyer, had blood tests taken, and all this other crap. None of it worked. This chick was completely psycho and now he is going to have a kid with her and there is nothing he can do. Poor guy. At press time, she had the baby. My buddy stopped going out. I haven't seen him in a year. I lost a good wingman. I really feel for the guy.

The first sign you get that a girl might be psycho, you need to cut off all relations. Avoid psycho chicks at all costs.

# IV. Inside Tips

## 64. Enjoy Your Toy

This is not a perverted tip about phallic symbols. This is a straightforward tip about enjoying your toys. The best way to describe this one is through a couple examples.

I have a buddy Jackie who was mired in a slump. It was spring. I was telling him not to worry about it; summer was right around the corner. Jackie was an options trader and he was getting his first big bonus from his company. The bonus turned out to be a very nice one, a little over $100k. What Jackie did with the money was smart. I was really proud of him. He didn't do anything stupid with the money like investing it or putting it into his savings. If he did that, he'd have to wait until he's married to enjoy it. Jackieboy went out and spent $110k on a new four-door black on black Maserati.

The car was so sick. Heads would turn wherever we went in it. We would valet it at the local nightclub and ropes would lift as soon as we walked up to go in. Chicks were noticing. Summer was just beginning. It was on.

After the brilliant move of buying the car instead of investing the money, Jackie did something very un-brilliant. He met some chick, not super hot, just attractive. They started dating, and he immediately moved into boyfriend/girlfriend mode with this chick. Complete lockdown. Say what!?! What a dummy! The summer was just beginning and he could have done some serious damage with that car. Here he goes spending all this money on this new toy and now he doesn't even get to enjoy it. Hence, enjoy your toy.

That brings to mind my buddy Stubby. Stubby got his nickname when some chick dumped her drink on him in a bar. He dated her briefly, then dumped her cold. He must have gone about it in a bad way because she was pissed. She ran into him in a bar, came over and started chewing him out. It was loud; the whole bar could hear. The line we all remembered was, "Who the fuck are you…you're a nobody…your terrible in bed, you short dick, stubby, piece of dogshit." Ouch! She dumped her drink on him and strutted out. It was cold-blooded man. We all laughed about it the next day. Somebody said, "Man, she called you 'Stubby' bro!" We called him Stubby the rest of the weekend and the name stuck.

After Stubby broke up with that chick he went on a dry spell. Then he did something smart. Stubby owned a phat top floor condo with roof rights. He stepped up and forked out some big dollars for an eight-man top-of-the-line jacuzzi. He hired an engineer to make the roof solid and secure. He hired a crane to put the jacuzzi on the roof. He built a full tiki bar up there. He put a ping pong table up there. Made the whole roof a party zone. It was a fricken sweet setup, perfect for summer parties or afterparties.

Stubby new my reputation and said it was up to me to get girls back to enjoy his new rooftop. I came through with flying colors. We had a party up there in the spring and it was off the hoooook! Full bar, two kegs, chicks everywhere, bumpin hip hop. Hip hop was blaring and chicks were getting drunk. Late night when the crowd dispersed we got a few poptarts in the hot tub. We were playing the game, 'I've never.' Chicks were making out with chicks, tops were coming off; it was great. Later on that night, I played Hide The Carrot with some cute little poptart down in Stubby's room. Came all over his sheets and had to buy him new ones.

Stubby hooked up with some chick too. Then Stubby completely blew it. He failed to enjoy his toy. Yep, he fell for that girl and started dating her and that was it. No more jacuzzi parties. No more afterparties. The rooftop went unused for the rest of summer. What a waste!

*Point of Advice: Do not buy a new toy if you are not prepared to take full advantage of it.*

The last sad story I have tell about this subject involves my buddy Carter. Carter was a really funny guy. He made all of us laugh. He was happy go lucky. He had dark hair, dimples, and about 40 extra pounds on his frame. One winter Carter hit the gym bigtime. By summertime he was a whole new man. We were all amazed and gave him lots of props. He looked great.

You know how this one is going to end. Carter was use to getting plump, rotund chicks. With his weight loss he had moved up from the JV team to the varsity team. He wasn't prepared. The first weekend we went out with our new & improved friend, he met a decent looking chick. She was no All-Star, but not bad. Carter hooked onto her and wouldn't let go. He dated her the entire summer. End of summer, they broke up. Carter wasted his whole summer with this broad! At least Carter learned his lesson. He continued to hit the gym and stay fit. Now he is wising up and enjoying his new self.

## 65. Hot and Cold Streaks

There will be times when you are going out and meeting a hot chick every night. You will be getting laid left and right. Your cell phone will be jam-packed with strange girl's names. You will even be turning down some chicks you might normally hook up with. These are hot streaks. There is nothing better. Hot streaks have the snowball effect in that other chicks somehow have this secret radar ability to know when a guy is getting laid a lot, and they covet these men. They sense that this guy has something going on, and they want to know more. When you are hot, chicks feel your vibe and you meet more chicks and it just snowballs.

There's a flip side to this. The inevitable cold streak. These do happen, and frankly, you just can't worry about them. Shrug them off and wait for a hot streak. The best gigolos and playboys in the world have dry spells. It's a fact of life. The same can be said for the best poker players, the best baseball players, the best car salesmen, the best stock traders, everybody. You have to battle through the cold streaks. You might even have to hook up with a slumpbuster or some chick you are not attracted to in order to overcome your dry spell. When you are in the middle of a cold streak, you have to tell yourself, "Self, I am in the middle of a cold streak and there is nothing wrong with that. Things will turn around soon; I just have to persevere." The only way to make it go by faster is to sharpen your skills and make sure you are doing everything correct. Re-read this book the next time you are in the middle of a cold streak. You'll get through your cold streak faster than a virgin on prom night.

## 66. Work Wool Here

I was in Vegas years ago with Party Scars, Giles, Roger, and Mexicuddler. We were staying at The Mirage for some dumb reason. We usually prefer The Palms, The Hard Rock, or Mandalay Bay because that's where all the young people and hot chicks stay and congregate.

We were wandering around the Mirage on a Saturday around 2pm. We were trying to figure out where to go. We wanted to hang out, find some chicks, and start partying. Everyone was throwing out ideas and no one could agree on anything. As we walked through the casino, everyone was getting frustrated. Suddenly Giles stopped, turned to us and said, "I've got it." He paused and then emphatically said, "Work wool heeeere!"

In this crude and simple revelation, Giles actually made a lot of sense. It was like wisdom in the simplest form had just knocked us on the head.

We all paused and thought about it. We began to look around. There were a bunch of old people gambling of course, but there were hot chicks sprinkled all around the casino. Giles was right, we needed to start working all the chicks around us. We ordered some drinks and then hit on some hillbilly chicks playing slot machines. Mexicuddler sat down and played some blackjack with two hot cougars. Roger and I approached two college chicks who looked lost and helped them find their way. Got their phone number in the process. We all began talking to chicks and it was on. Next thing we knew it was nighttime and we had a bunch of chicks meeting us out that night. I'd never heard that phrase before, but now "Work wool here" is embedded in my mind. **Work chicks wherever you are, whenever the opportunity presents itself.**

Now I 'work wool' just about anywhere. Hot chicks have their guard up at nightclubs, bars, and the gym. However, they have their guard *down* at the mall, movies, weddings, bookstores, Blockbuster, gay parades, hair shows, walking down the street, offices, grocery stores, airports, and more.

The mall: it's easy to meet chicks at the mall. Chicks love shopping just about as much as men love pussy. Therefore, chicks are always in great moods when they are at the mall. Because they are in such happy spirits, they are easy to approach. It's easy to strike up a conversation and make them laugh. You can use the simple line, "Do you like this shirt?" or "Excuse me, but do you like this cologne?" Hey, anything works as an opener in the mall. Just step up to the plate and you will see how easy it is to meet chick in a mall.

Movies: Girls love romantic comedies, and when they come out of the movie they are feeling romantic. They are definitely guy-friendly after they've seen a romantic comedy. They are in the perfect frame of mind to be hit on. My buddy Gooch & I worked this bar next to the movie theatre for a good solid year and we got plenty of tail doing it.

Weddings: Chicks love weddings! A chick watching a man & woman get married makes her want a man for herself. Immediately! Want to make a horny cocktail? Throw in one part wedding, two parts alcohol. You'll have one horny chick on your hands.

Bookstores: The best thing about picking up chicks in a bookstore is that there is always something to talk about. It is easy to approach a chick in a bookstore and ask her a question about whatever book she is looking at. Bookstores are great places to have conversations with new chicks.

Blockbuster: Hitting on chicks in Blockbuster is easy. I've done it before and been successful. It is not my favorite though. Most of the chicks renting movies are fat or ugly. It's the law of nature that more fat or ugly chicks rent movies because they don't have guys taking them out on dates. Hotter chicks rent fewer movies because they are busier. Furthermore, many of the hot chicks who do rent movies are there with guys. Thus, I wouldn't make Blockbuster a destination for picking up chicks like I would these other venues. Besides, leaving your house to rent a movie will be a thing of the past soon.

Gay Parades: Gay parades are an untapped channel for meeting chicks. I have been to half a dozen gay parades and hooked up with a hot chick *every time*. It is that easy! First of all, more than anywhere else, chicks have their guard down at gay parades. They think there is no way some horny dude like myself would show up to a gay parade trying to swoop down on unsuspecting chicks. Second, all the gay dudes there are flirting will all the other gay dudes, so this makes the chicks want to flirt also. Third, there are a lot of women at gay parades, and very few straight guys, so you are a hot commodity. Fourth, chicks like and respect a guy who is comfortable enough with his sexuality to attend a gay parade. Fifth, you can fuck with chicks and tell them that you aren't sure about your sexuality. This drives them crazy and leads to women wanting you so they can taste that forbidden fruit. Gay parades are a goldmine for pussy! I am pounding the table on this one!

Walking down the street: The best thing about picking up on a chick walking down the street is that it takes a man with big balls to approach a random chick walking down the street. After she gets over the surprise of being approached by a random guy, she will initially be flattered. She will also be impressed.

Offices: Women also have their guard down at work. This is a great time to flirt. Flirting in an office environment is a great way to set up future hook ups. Caution though, it is not advised to hook up with a co-worker whom you deal with on a daily basis. Humping and dumping a co-worker can lead to office friction.

Grocery stores: When I lived in San Francisco, I worked wool at the Safeway grocery store in the Marina district like it was a nightclub on a Saturday night. The place always had sexy, young chicks grocery shopping. They were totally open to being hit on. Many grocery stores are similar. Eye-contact is an important ingredient for working chicks in a grocery store. If I make eye-contact with an attractive woman on aisle 4, I make sure that we coincidentally meet up again on aisle 6. Then I just throw out a comment or something. That leads to chit-chat and then I'll just be forward and say, "You know, I am very good cook, and we live pretty close to each other….would you be open to letting me cook you dinner one night?" Keep in mind that I can't cook a fricken hot dog, let alone a full course meal, but I would cross that bridge when I came to it. My only concern was getting her to agree to see me again. When it works,

I order some catered food from a top notch restaurant. If she bothers to ask, "Did you really cook this?" I come clean and tell her the truth. She laughs. I get laid. All is good.

Another note about picking up chicks in grocery stores is to be aware of what's in her shopping cart. If she is buying frozen meals, healthy food, and Cosmo magazine, she is a perfect target. But if she is buying any of the following, here is what pops in my head: mens deodorant (boyfriend), baby food (milf), bratwurst (fat), cheap beer (boyfriend), a pregnancy test (slut), frozen pizzas (fat), Ben & Jerrys (fat and lonely), Preparation H (not healthy), condoms (slut), etc. Pay attention to what's in her shopping cart.

Airports: Airports are another great place to meet women. Women are always in a good mood because they are traveling. They have a lot on their mind - none of which has to do with meeting a nice guy. Therefore, you can catch them off guard by just being friendly and striking up a conversation. You never know what can happen after that.

## 67. Cougars

Watch out for cougars! A cougar is a rare breed of woman. In case you are unclear on the definition of a Cougar, here it is: A cougar is a woman, 30-45, dressing and acting like she is in her early twenties. Age alone does not classify a female as a cougar. What distinguishes a cougar from other women is their aggressive and fearless nature. Cougars are often on the prowl for young men, actively hunting them down and having their way with them. Cougars know what they want and they usually aren't shy about it. They can be brash, cunning and persuasive.

A cougar can capture you, take you home, fuck your brains out, and all you wake up to is her business card on your pillow. Yeah, cougars roll like that. I've experienced it firsthand.

Young women are not cougars because they still prefer to be pursued, they are still worried what their girlfriends might think, and they are still a little naïve. Men cannot be cougars because men are horny and aggressive from 16 till 75. That is why cougars are a phenomena. Many women do not hit their sexual peek until their early 30s. By this time many are divorced, or they've been through many rough relationships. They have seen it all. If they want a man, they won't make it a secret. This is why you will often see older women staring at you. They might approach you. They might even offer to buy you a drink. They wear seductive clothing that is longer in style. They look a little out of place but they make it well known they are single and available.

Now all this being said, many of my friends have a big weakness for cougars. Nothin wrong with that! Cougars can satisfy many hungers.

You can now consider yourself forewarned about cougars.

Side note here. My buddy Fat Matt in San Francisco is actually the one who coined the term 'cougar.' He faxed us a diagram one day while he was bored at work showing how a girl evolves into a cougar. Cougar made everyone laugh. I travel a lot and spread the term to my SoCal crew and my Chicago crew. Fat Matt knows a lot of people too and the term just spread like wildfire. Now it is well known. Some of the young 22 year-old chicks I date hear me say 'Cougar' and they will ask me what a 'Cougar' is. Poptarts love hearing the explanation.

Side note II: My buddy Scott says that it is mandatory to yell out, "Cougarrr!" every time you happen to see a cougar. I don't necessarily subscribe to this rule, but I do participate occasionally.

## 68. Foreign Women

I highly recommend dating foreign women. One major reason to pursue foreign women is their attitude. Frankly, there are a lot of American chicks out there with bad attitudes. You might not realize this until you visit a foreign country. Foreign women treat their man like a king. Foreign women are not stuck up or conceited the way many American biatches are. Women from other countries have respect for their man. In some foreign countries women outnumber the men. Therefore, the woman realizes a good man is hard to find. In America, some chick will think she is so hot and her shit doesn't stink. You might be dating her and the whole time she is acting like she will dump you in a heartbeat if you don't treat her like a princess. Not so with foreign women. They are happy to be with you and they consider themselves lucky.

Another reason to date foreign women is they are more traditional and old-fashioned. They are more apt to cook you dinner every night, do your laundry, suck your dick, pick you up from the airport, anything to make you happy. If a chick starts cooking dinner for me on a regular basis, it moves her way up the scale in my book. To get an American chick to cook you dinner is like pulling teeth nowadays.

Foreign women in general are in better shape. Did you know America is the fattest country in the world?! This is pathetic. I don't give fat chicks the time of day. I have no respect for them. I hate it when you see some decent looking overweight American broad with an attitude. She must have been hit on by too many desperate guys or something and now she is all stuck up and pompous. That is why I ignore all fat chicks. If they had any zest for life they would stop cramming double cheeseburgers down their throat and get themselves in shape.

Another bonus that comes with dating foreign women are the great things you will learn about her home country.

I love learning about the culture in Poland or Brazil or Denmark. This is cool. It has even helped me meet other chicks from that country on down the line. I learned so much about Poland after dating this hot Polish broad for a couple months. Then I would be in Chicago where there is a large Polish population. I would spot a Polish chick and say hello to her in her native language. Dzien dobry. She would be surprised, and a conversation would ensue. She would love it that I was knowledgeable about her country, and that's all I needed to hook up with her or get her digits.

Last but not least, don't forget the accents. You gotta love a sexy foreign accent, it's a major turn on. This alone is reason enough to date foreign chicks.

## 69. The Real World Generation

Young girls are much more liberal about sex these days. Let me tell ya brother! They are down for just about anything! They are opened minded and willing to try everything once. Many girls feel obligated to have a threesome just for the simple fact that when their friends ask, "Have you ever been in a threesome," they don't have to give an embarrassing, "No," answer. Isn't that great?!

The reason this whole generation became daring and promiscuous...well it was MTV. It started with all the hoochie-mammas shaking their bootie in every hip hop video you see. Then there was Britney Spears evolving into a slut on in front of our very eyes. But by far the main culprit for this evolution was The Real World. This show revolutionized an entire generation to start having more sex, and wilder sex. I can even name the season. It was The Real World Las Vegas. Ever since then girls think it is the norm to be sleeping with multiple partners, girls kissing girls, getting naked all the time, sex in public, and more! This a great news for us guys, and I personally welcomed this revolution with open arms. So understand that young girls aren't naïve. They are probably down for a wild & crazy night if the situation presents itself.

If you get a sense that a girl might be going through her sexually adventurous stage, don't be shy about pushing the envelope. Often times I bring up borderline subjects while I am talking to a young Real World Generation girl. I'll even ask, straight up, if she has ever been in a threesome. If she says yes, I know I have a chick on my hands who likes to party. If she says, "Mmmm no," in a manner where I can tell she is curious, then I know I have a chick who might want to party. I'll do my best to make it happen. Gotta love the new generation.

## 70. New Guy In Town

In these modern days it is likely you will live & work in different cities throughout your career. I have lived in half a dozen different cities. Being the new guy in town is great.

As the new guy in town, you are completely free. There are no ex-girlfriends, retreads, ex-one night stands, or anything like that to worry about. There are new bars to discover, new nightclubs, new stripclubs, new restaurants, new friends to meet, and, of course, new women. Getting a fresh start in a new city really is exhilarating.

But the best thing about being the new guy in town is how appealing it is to females. Women love the new guy in town! The new guy in town is definitely single, no strings attached. If you had a girlfriend or wife, you'd be with her right now, not out at the bars. There are lots of places the new guy doesn't know about. Chicks would love to be the one to show you around. The new guy in town always has a lot of energy. He carries a vacation-type mentality, and women are attracted to that. Furthermore, single chicks are probably tired of the same ole guys they see out every weekend. They want some fresh blood! A new guy in town can be different and mysterious and fun.

I will milk that new guy role for a while. I might be living there for ten months, but I'll still tell girls I just moved here. Even though I may know a great deal about the city, I'll act naïve. I want to relish my new guy status for as long as possible. Heck, sometimes when I travel to Vegas, LA, anywhere, I tell chicks I just moved there. They love the New Guy that much. I dated a smoking hot waitress in Vegas for two months before she found out I didn't even live there.

When I moved back to San Diego, I played the new guy role for a whole year. My first summer there was pussy over-load. I was living in Pacific Beach. PB is one of the all time great young neighborhoods in America. A beach town with hot chicks everywhere. One night we all went out to Stinga-ree in downtown San Diego. I met this cute blond. She was pretty decent, maybe a 7. She was a rich daddy's girl. I gave her some attitude and then I was nice to her. It worked. She was into me. She lived in PB too, just a few blocks from my place. We flirted with each other, grabbed a little ass, and then her friends whisked her away. They were going to another night-club. I gave her my number and my address so we could hook up in the future. I stayed at Stingaree and kept working the new guy angle. I found this brunette Latin chick who wanted to party. We flirted for a while. We both downed a shot of Patron at the bar. She was cool. Place was closing so I coerced back to my house in PB. We took a long cab ride home. By the time we got back she was starting to sober up. We kissed for a while. I played with her boobs but then she put the brakes on. She said she had to go. She called a cab and ten minutes later she was gone. Dammit!

I retired to my bedroom.

I had the front bedroom of an old three bedroom house.

That night I had met some hot chicks, but still didn't get laid. Time to rub one off. I was laying in my bed, getting worked up, ready to rub one off, when....

Boom! Boom, Boom!!!

A huge thumping on my bedroom window! I jumped two feet in the air, cock in hand, scared shitless.

The blond daddy's girl from earlier in the night was banging on my screen and window. She was drunk. She said, "Billy? Billy, are you in there?" I said, "Uh...yeah." She said, "Can I come in?"

I thought for a second. My first instinct was, "Dammit, I was really looking forward to beating off right now." Then I thought, "Wait a minute, what am I thinking? This chick can only be here for one reason."

I said, "Yeah, the front door is open. Come in here." She came in my room. The lights were off. She just hopped in my bed. We started making out. I guided her hand and put it on my cock. She said, "Wow, you get hard really fast." We fooled around. She said, "No, we shouldn't," a few times, and then we had sex.

## 71. Working The Net

Having an online presence is becoming increasingly important. A Myspace page or a Facebook page is necessary nowadays. Not for meeting chicks, but for letting them see you are a normal guy.

I never meet chicks online. I meet them face to face out in the real world. Many times it's a chance encounter at a bar and we are both drunk. I don't remember exactly what she looks like and she probably feels the same. If I can send her a message through Myspace, she can check out my page, look at photos of me, check out my interests, etc. This is very important! It lets her know I am normal. I don't have 4000 Myspace friends. I don't have porno chick friends. I don't have satanic symbols on my page. I just have a cool write-up and lots of photos of my friends and me laughing and partying. This is very comforting to a girl. Before, it would take one or two dates for her to figure out that you're a normal guy and not an ax murderer. Now, she can visit your Myspace page and feel worry-free about hanging out with you. If you have a cool enough page, it can make her desire your company even more.

I am not a big fan of online dating; it's just not my cup of tea. But I won't castigate it. I know people that swear by it. There are some guys who do very well on Yahoo Personals, Match.com, and others. My buddy Grady is one of those guys. He's always nailing chicks from Match.com. They aren't the hottest chicks, but they are chicks, and they are horny. He also did very well on eHarmony.com. He said that website was the easiest of them all. Every chick on there is dying to find a husband and get married. They are desperate and eager to please. The last thing Grady wants to do is get married. But he acted like he did. He said by the second date it was guaranteed sex. Sometimes the first date. The women are so eager to please their man, they put out right away. But it's only good for three of four dates before the girls start talking serious and become too attached. Then he moves on. Put a guy like me on that website and look out. I'd go through that site like a hot knife through butter. Poor girls wouldn't stand a chance.

Not for me though. I enjoy the chase too much.

## 72.  Nice To Have A Mentor

No matter what you are trying to improve, it's always nice to have a mentor or a teacher. If you have a friend in your crew who scores a lot, try to emulate what works for him.

My early road trips with Giles and other buddies were great learning experiences for me. Giles was a close friend who had the uncanny ability to get smoking hot chicks to fall in love with him in just one night. He was the best I have ever seen, maybe even better than me. I learned a great deal from him. Giles had a look to him that no one else had. He wasn't ugly, wasn't good looking. He had long shoulder-length hair that was dark black and very curly. Girls loved his hair. Guys wanted to kick his ass cause of it. He also dressed differently. He wore linen all the time and white pants and jewelry and shit like that. I mean who wears linen?

The first time I ever hung out with him was on a Lake Tahoe road trip with mutual friends. I was still wet behind the ears and he was a seasoned expert. We went out that night and I was use to hanging out on the sidelines, hoping some chick would stare at me. I was so green. He did his now patented move, the hand grab, where he grabs some chick's hand firmly and pulls her in and says I don't know what, but it must be good…. It is so bold and daring that when it works, it works very well. When it doesn't work, chicks chew him out. He doesn't care; it works more often than it doesn't. In Tahoe I watched him grab the hottest chick in the bar, this exotic half white, half Spanish chick with a perfect rack, nice Angelina Jolie lips, and reddish brown hair. She was a 10. I was awestruck.

He swung her around on the dance floor, bought her some drinks, and spoke to her for a half hour. She fell in love with him. We ended up back at our cabin. The three of us buddies had to listen to Giles tap that ass all night. The headboard was pounding on the wall and we could all hear it - he must have been really killing it. What a performance by Giles. I was thoroughly impressed.

The next night we went out to the same place, and there she is. Tahoe is a small town, so no big surprise to see her again. I was still amazed at how sexy and exotic this woman was. Giles straight up ignored her. He hooked up with the 2nd hottest chick in the bar. A solid 9. I was stunned. I thought he would be so happy to see her and he would again spend the evening with her. I was so naïve. I pulled him aside later and said, "G, that chick you were with last night is over there, and she keeps staring at you." He said, "I know. She is so high maintenance though, and she has crooked teeth. You can go get on her if you want."

I was blown away. I thought, 'Holy crap he is turning down this chick?!' Giles brought the second girl back to our cabin that night. I had to listen to the headboard banging against the wall all night again. Giles had gone two-for-two on this short weekend road trip. Truly a magnificent feat. That weekend was a big influence on my future. Giles & I would go on to become very close friends. We still are to this day. Years later he would tell me that that was an exceptional weekend, even for him.

We were in Vegas with a few buddies. It was a couple years later. I had come a long way since my naïve days in Tahoe. I was now a Level 9 Master Gigolo. Giles was still a 10, but I was hot on his heels. We went out that night in Vegas and again he brought back a smoking hot chick. A brunette nursing student from Sacramento. She was fine; she looked like Winona Ryder, but taller and hotter. I hooked up but couldn't close the deal, so I was stuck in the room late night.

I was doing the Army Crawl, hiding near the base of the bed while G tried to get laid. G was drunk, his girl was really drunk, and I was spinning wasted drunk.

G got her naked. He didn't know I was in the room until he got up to take a pee and stepped on me. He started to crack up but then caught himself. He was being cool and letting me reach up there and play with her boobs while she wasn't paying attention. It was dark and she thought it was G's hand. He fooled around with her some more. At one point he was kissing her nice ass, literally, and I popped up from the floor. He had both hands on her ass; she was on all fours. He was looking at her nice ass like it was the Holy Grail or something. When I popped up, he quietly giggled and showed me her perfect ass. He nodded for me to rub her ass. So I put my index finger in my mouth, and then, in a corkscrew twisting motion, stuck my finger in her bunghole. She yelped and jumped forward six inches. It made a sound like when you put your index finger sideways in your mouth and then pop your finger out of your cheek; that's what it sounded like. G didn't know I was going to do that (I didn't know I was going to do that).

He continued to fool around with her. She must have known I was in the room. I army crawled over to the door and opened and shut it and walked in and pretended like I had just arrived home. They were under the sheets. There was only one bed, so I said I would sleep on the floor. G knew it was time for him to get down to business. They started having sex. I got really turned on and tried to get involved. I got up on the bed next to her, grabbed her hand and put it on my johnson (I was naked). She grabbed it and started stroking it. I was pretty happy that she was so receptive & hospitable. This was cool for a while, but then I wanted to do what G was doing. He was on top of her pounding her. I was hammered but I now had a full hard-on and wanted to bone her! I scooted down and whispered to G, "Hey let me in there." I said it again. Got no response.

Play time was over and Giles was having none of that. He ignored me. So I decided I would try to get her to suck my dick. It was dark as hell in there. She was petite, and G's fricken hair was so long that I couldn't see much of her. I got up there and put it near her mouth, and finally found her mouth. She must have had her head tilted way back somehow and I was glad to be getting something. But she wasn't putting it in her mouth, she was just letting me stroke it on her lips back and forth. I had one hand on the wall and I was looking at the wall and G was pummeling her missionary. The room started spinning again because I was so drunk. I said fuck this, there is no way I can cum from this. So I backed off and went and passed out in the corner on the floor.

The next day G went with her and dropped her off at her hotel. We met up later for dinner. The four of us on the trip were laughing and telling stories from the previous night. One of the other guys on the trip got laid also, and he was telling us about it. Then I was telling them how I fingered G's chick's bunghole and I showed them the sound it made and we all laughed. G nodded his head in laughter and said "Yep, that's what it sounded like." That was a good laugh. I went on to tell them how she was sucking my dick for a little while, while G was drilling her missionary. That's when G stopped me and his smile gradually turned to a frown. He informed us of what really happened. Apparently, under all the hair and darkness and drunkness, that wasn't her mouth. G said that I was nowhere near her mouth. He said he had his hands under her head, and his arms were at a 90 degree angle. Somehow I thought *his* inner-elbow was *her* mouth, and I was fucking my buddy's inner arm. Whoops! He said I was going to ruin his sex if I would have kept doing it. Fortunately, I only did that for a minute or two. The other guys got a big laugh out of that one.

One last story about Giles. We have come a long way since that weekend in Tahoe. I moved away, down to San Diego, but we kept in touch often and went on road trips once or twice a year. Giles ended up moving to Europe with this really cool beautiful blond Euro chick and began settling down. I was the opposite. I went hogwild in Southern California and took my gigolo skills to another level.

We went two years without seeing each other, so I flew out to Amsterdam to hang with my good bro for a weekend. He got a hall-pass from his chick, so he drove in from Germany for the weekend. We got a hotel room in Amsterdam. It was really great seeing him. We gave each other big hugs at the airport, checked into the hotel, showered up early, and hit the town. Giles wasn't use to going out since he lived with his chick. He was pretty mellow. We stayed away from the red-light district in Amsterdam (it's nasty there) and found some cool café/restaurant. We ordered some food and a bottle of red vino. We started talking about, what else, pussy. I was telling him about some of my wilder escapades in SoCal. He was listening intently and loving it. Then he would tell me about one of his former conquests. We went back and forth trading war stories for two or three hours. I kept laughing and so did Giles. We went through two bottles of wine. It was such a good fricken time trading stories with my bro who I hadn't seen in such a long time, and talking about our favorite subject, chasing tail.

It was dark when we decided to leave, around 10pm. With a good buzz, we stepped out onto the street. We had no plans. We walked a couple blocks and passed by a Dutch bar called Three Sisters. There was good music coming from inside so we stopped and went in. This little hole in the wall bar was crowded! In the back there was even a makeshift dancefloor and people were dancing to American hip hop. Sweet!

We grabbed two Heinekens and went to the back of the bar. We finished our first beer so G went to get us another round. Across the floor I noticed a really pretty, young looking brunette. She was a solid 9 at least, pale, no makeup, tight body, and very innocent. She was dancing with her friend and really getting into it. She was dancing all over the place, with a lot of enthusiasm. I could tell she was a young college student who rarely went out. She looked so innocent and hot. Her dark hair and pale skin reminded me of Snow White. I wanted to drill her seven times.

G came back and I said, "G, G! See that girl way over there? Look at how she is dancing. See all the energy she has; *that* girl is going to give somebody a great blowjob later on tonight…"

I hadn't yet finished my sentence when Giles was already on his way over there. I was like, 'Damn!' I wanted to drink another beer or two before I made a move, but not G.

Never hesitate. G moved right through all the passive Dutch guys watching her dance, grabbed her by the hand, spun her around a couple times like swing-dancing, and he was in. She didn't know what hit her. G danced with her & her friend and they were having a blast. He motioned for me to come over, but her friend was beat, and I was sober, so I declined.

I was still hanging out on the sidelines across the bar with my thumb up my ass. I thought my game had come a long way, but apparently G was still the grandmaster of picking up chicks. Twenty minutes went by. Two chicks and a dude came over and started dancing near me. The second girl wasn't dancing though, she was just hanging close to her girlfriend. She was quiet, blond, low cut top, perfect Eastern European boobs, sexy cleavage, and a very cute face. It looked like her friend had met a guy, but not her. I leaned over and said, "Are you not in the dancing mood?" She turned to see who was talking to her, then said, "No, not right now." I was prepared and quickly responded back, "I need to be a little intoxicated before I dance, then I don't care what I look like." I smiled. She smiled back and looked at me again, "Where are you from?" She could tell I had a foreign accent, which was good because I love telling chicks I am American.

We hit it off right away.

It didn't take long before I got her in the corner and we were making out. I was holding her firmly and we were really kissing passionately. I began rubbing those perfect boobs. Oh man she had some nice melons.

We finished another cocktail and then I told her that my hotel was around the corner and she should 'come see my view of the river, then we can come back.' It took a lot of coercion, but it worked. I got her out of the bar and back to my little third-floor dumpy hotel room. It was on the 3rd floor of four, up these old creaky Dutch stairs. We got there and began kissing and removing clothing. We got buck naked. She had an incredible body. I was playing with her boobs and it was time to put on a condom.

I was trying to find my rubbers when….I had to pause. I listened. We could hear those old creaky stairs. Somebody was coming up. The doorknob began to jiggle so I jumped back in the bed. But the covers were off so we were both buck-naked on this narrow twin bed.

The door opened. Giles and Snow White walked in and flicked on the lights.

They were both very surprised to see us in the room, and even more shocked that we were naked, me holding a condom.

Immediately, I realized the magnitude of the situation. I had scored first! I was thinking of how funny it would be to talk to G about it tomorrow. G didn't say a word, but looked at me for a split second with a look of like, 'Wow.' Obe One then looked at Young Skywalker with great admiration. He turned back down the stairs with his girl and walked away.

G and his girl left for an hour or two. My girl and I got it on a couple times. She was great in bed, and actually wanted to go a third time, but I knew G needed the room. We left and G and his girl came walking back at exactly the right time.

The next day at breakfast G was saying, "Holy shit dude, I saw you hanging out by the wall by yourself. Then a half-hour later you are banging some hot chick!?!" (It was probably more like an hour) Giles continued, "I go to take my girl to the hotel room, and you are already up there naked & scoring!?!" "I couldn't believe it Billy. How did you work her so fast?"

You don't know how much satisfaction I got from my former mentor saying that! Not only that, but I love shocking others with my scoring abilities. It was a hell of good night. Two hours of trading war stories over some cheap French wine with my close friend, then both of us scoring with hot chicks, and both of us laughing about it the next day. Doesn't get much better…

## 73. Never Bring Sand To The Beach

You ever see those guys that show up to a bar, club, or party with a bunch of single chicks? It happens often. I'm glad it does, more chicks for me! But bringing chicks to the club is not how I roll. Just not my style. I am there to meet girls, not hang out with girls I already know. It just doesn't make sense to bring sand to the beach. Maybe these girls are brought along as friends, or co-workers, or chicks these guys want to scam on, or chicks they have already had sex with. As you will see, all of these scenarios are bad news.

If I bring female friends or co-workers to some bar, they aren't going to see much of me. I am going to be roaming around trying to hook up with other chicks. I'm not going to waste my time talking to some female friends when there are hot little horny poptarts running around. Bringing these friends can also lead to me developing a bad reputation. I might do some shady things they don't approve of. Therefore, I rarely if ever bring female friends or co-workers to a place where I want to meet women.

Bringing a girl you know and with whom you are hoping to hook up with to a bar/nightclub is also a bad idea. First of all, you can't scam on any other chicks - you are basically in lockdown, and that is no fun. Also, you have to be on your best behavior and that is hard to do in a poppin nightclub full of hotties.

Don't forget, there are many guys there, who, if you leave your girl alone for a minute, will pounce on her. It's a pain in the ass trying to fight off all the other vultures at a nightclub.

Lastly, if you bring some chick you've already had sex with, you two will either be the boring people hanging out in the corner, or you and/or she will be flirting with other people and that will lead to unwanted fireworks.

This is why I *never* bring sand to the beach.

# 74. Be Seen With Hot Chicks

Being seen in the presence of hot women will attract other women. This is an ironic fact of life. You become desirable. You become mysterious. You become sought-after. Women will stare at you and wonder what attributes you have that make other women want to hang out with you. Just the fact that a good-looking female is with you or talking to you makes other women curious. Subconsciously, the decision of whether or not you are attractive has already been made! The decision of whether or not you are worth talking to has already been made. This removes barriers that women put up to fend of other men. Once these barriers are removed, it is easy to meet, talk to, and hook up with these women.

Stand in a bar or club and hangout with your buddies and you probably won't get much love. But get involved in an engaging conversation with a hot girl and suddenly a lot of women will be checking you out. Women are stimulated and turned-on by a man in the presence of an attractive woman. This creates opportunities. In *The Art Of War*, Sun Tzu wrote "Opportunities multiply as they are seized." When you seize the opportunity of talking to a hot chick, other chicks take notice, and this leads to more opportunities, and more hot chicks.

This is why you go out some nights and you are on fire, meeting girl after girl, and other nights girls won't give you the time of day. Talking to and being seen with hot women is not easy but, once accomplished, it has a snowball effect. This is also why some guys bring sand to the beach. I disagree with that move, but I can understand the motive. Instead of bringing them there, meet them there. That will give you more freedom.

## 75. Never Wait In Line

Never wait in line. It is just not worth it. When you calculate it all out, you'll see that your time is too valuable to wait in line. It usually only takes $20 bucks per person to grease most bouncers or doormen. You'll be in the nightclub for three to five hours. Are you are going to spend one of those hours outside waiting in line? Hell no.

Don't look at it like you are spending extra money to get in sooner, look at it like you are *saving* $20 bucks by waiting outside in line for an hour. Do you really want to save $20 dollars that badly? I think not.

Paying $20 bucks extra to be in the proximity of eligible, horny, young females an hour earlier seems worth it, right? Paying $20 bucks extra to be in a bar having a cocktail, hanging with your buddies, listening to music and hour earlier seems worth it, right? So step up and pay the extra $20 or $40 or whatever. Let those other jackoffs wait in line. In NYC and Miami you might have to pay a little more, maybe a $100 bucks, but it will still be worth it.

A further benefit is that you might be spotted getting past the line by some hot chicks, or by some goldiggers, and they will remember you once you are in. I paid $20 to get past a ten-minute line in Dallas one time. Some fake-boobed golddigger noticed. She was all over me inside because she thought I was a high roller - it was an easy score. So do your best to skip the line.

## 76. Grease the Doorman

Never approach a random doorman. You have to figure out who the head doorguy is, or which guy has the VIP list. There are usually only two guys outside, so it's easy to tell which one of them is the right guy to talk to, and which guy is clueless. I often see knuckleheads approach some random doorman who has no pull at all. Approach the proper doorman, and do it with confidence. He won't know if you are some VIP or what, so he will respond to you; act like a VIP. Sometimes I have even had to motion him over. Whatever you do, just do it with confidence like you own the place. When he comes next to you, act like you are about to shake his hand, and then look down at your hand at the last second. He will too. Have the $20 or $40 or $100 folded and showing the big 20 sign (Not folded so he can't tell if it's a $5 bill or $20 bill). As soon as he makes eye-contact with the money say this, "There are just two of us." Don't say anything else; no need for long explanations. This will work 90% of the time.

Never say, "How much buddy?" Never say, "Let me in guy." Assholes never get it.

Another option is to say, "I'm not sure if I'm on the list, will $50 get me to the front of the line?" Then hand him the money. Be aggressive in handing him the money. Don't wait for him to reach for it. Put the money in his hand so he barely has to move to accept it.

Another tip is saying how many are with you. If there are three of you total, always say "There are just two of us." You are implying two more of us, but he will just understand two total. It's a little play on words. Then when there are actually three of you are coming in he won't care about the extra person; he's already got your money in his pocket. So remember, if there are four of you, say, "Just three."

One more thing, with groups of 4 or more guys, do not crowd around the head doorguy. Have your buddies stand ten feet away, then motion for them when the time is right. Eight guys crowding the door will never get in.

If you are with girls, that obviously makes it much easier. But who brings sand to the beach?

## 77. Order A Stiff Drink

Sometimes a watered down, two-second pour cocktail just won't do. Sometimes you need a stiff drink for one reason or another. However, telling the bartender to pour you a strong drink could piss him/her off and make you look like a jerk. And asking for a double will cost you double.

Here is a quick little tip to use when you need a strong drink. I say this to the bartender after I have ordered: "Hurt me," or "Hurt me bro!" A little eye-contact and a smile are thrown in. That line is *very* effective. You're not being an asshole and you're not being greedy, you're just being a guy who wants to get his drink on. Bartenders can appreciate that. It's just a good way to casually let the bartender know that a strong drink would make you happy. Hurt me!

# 78.  Bar Trick With A Cherry

I've heard of some good bar tricks, but I think most of them make you look like you are trying too hard. Especially the ones where you need a prop like a deck of cards or some crap like that. Here is a low key one that I have used a couple times.

When the chick is not looking, I take a cherry from the bar where all the condiments are (limes, lemon peels, etc). I remove the stem off the cherry and tie it in a knot. Then I put that stem in my mouth under my tongue. I resume talking to the girl. Nonchalantly, I tell her I can do wonders with my tongue. Not only will this get her curious about what the trick is, but, subliminally, it will peak her sexual interest since you are talking about doing something with your tongue.

While she is watching, I reach and grab a new whole cherry and stem, I tilt my head back, and drop the entire thing in my mouth. I chew and swallow the cherry. With my mouth closed, I slide the 2nd stem under my tongue and pull out the first stem. It's tied neatly in a knot! I show her and say, "Look, I tied it in a knot with my tongue." No doubt she is impressed! She thinks I tied that little stem in a knot with just my tongue. Yeah right! But it is a good trick.

Then 10 minutes later, after we are hitting it off, I tell her my secret. She loves the joke and now I have her laughing and I am in, hopefully....

## 79. The Perfect Buzz

Listen, I love to go out boozing. It's one of my favorite things to do. I hesitated to even write about this because I love boozing so much. But getting *too* drunk ruins your chances of scoring. The Number One Reason Guys Don't Score With Chicks: They are too timid. That was an easy one. The Number Two Reason: They get too fucked up.

Yes, getting too drunk is that much of a mistake.

Everything starts out fine. People who are drinking are boisterous, outgoing, and fun to be around. But they'll hit that perfect buzz and keep on going. I did that for years. My brother still does it. He sails right on through the Perfect Buzz and into Belligerent Drunk. Guys who are too drunk cannot carry a conversation with girls. They cannot impress a girl with their personality. They surely cannot score. Belligerent drunks scare girls away. They slur their words and stumble around and make bad decisions. What a turn-off!

Now, as soon as I realize I have a good buzz going, I slow down. I want to maintain that perfect buzz. If I am taking a piss and my piss is clear, not yellow, I know I am drunk. I switch to beer. I might switch to water. I might keep on drinking cocktails, but much more slowly. I slow down because pussy is more important than alcohol.

Drink until you are drunk, and then slow down. Too many knuckleheads drink and drink and keep on drinking and do shot after shot. Late night when chicks are drunk and horny, those guys are incapacitated. Not me though. I'll still have a nice buzz, but I'll be thinking clearly, and I'll be ready to swoop down on all the wounded gazelles running around.

## 80. Forgetting Her Name

Every guy I know who parties forgets chick's names. I have been called out on it many times, yet the girl is still willing to hook up with me. I've woken up next to girls and not known their names numerous times. It's not a big deal. If you are concerned about forgetting a chick's name, here is a little trick I use. I say, "Can I call you sometime?" and then, before she can answer, I hand her my cell phone. She enters her name & number in my phone and now I got it.

Another way: while you are putting her digits in your phone, say "What is the correct spelling of your name?" Then she will spell it out and you're off the hook.

This is probably the least important tip in this book. I have scored with dozens of broads and never remembered their name from the getgo. Names are not important.

## 81. The Two Rule

Shy guys never score. Get the dream out of your head where you are hanging out in the club, chilling by the wall, some chick approaches you and tells you you're cute. That just never happens brother.

Chicks will not recognize you as being shy; they will recognize you as being chickenshit and insecure.

A lack of confidence is a turnoff. Take a chance and roll up and say Hi to a girl. At least once or twice a night. Everybody has a little shyness in them. Suppress those shy tendencies! I can't tell you how many times I have *forced* myself to go up and talk to some chick, only to say something stupid, and get turned away. So what! I have also had numerous times where I have went over, said something stupid, and the chick has responded favorably. Either she was in a talkative mood, or she was giving me props for coming over and hitting on her, or maybe she did think I was cute. Who knows?

I would rather make an ass out of myself than be the shy guy in the corner. I would rather hook up with a less than attractive girl than nothing at all. I have a lot more respect for a dude who hits on and takes home a fat chick rather than a dude who sits by the wall all night with his thumb up his ass. Shy guys are not an asset.

If you are shy, this must be overcome. Not all at once, but gradually. Start with the Two Rule. No matter how shy you are, tell yourself that every time you go out, you are going to talk to at least *two* women that night. I don't care what they look like, or what you say. It could be one sentence and you walk away. But no more shy, wallflower nights.

My buddy Oliver was shy. He was a colleague from work. Oliver liked going out with us because we made him laugh and we always hooked up with chicks. But Oliver never talked to chicks and never scored. He was not an asset. I told him if he wanted to continue to roll out with us, he had to follow the Two Rule. He had to talk to at least two chicks a night. Even if it was just a one liner and he got shot down, that would be fine; at least he would be making an effort. He told me, "But Billy, I don't know what to say." I told him, "Say this to every girl: 'I think you are special.'" She will respond with, "Oh really, why do you think that?" Then you say, "You just seem down-to-earth." (All chicks *think* they are down-to-earth.) I told him after that he was on his own. If she is interested in you at all, she will make an effort to continue the conversation.

Oliver forced himself to do that. The first night it worked *both* times. After a few weekends out with us, Oliver met a chick he liked and they started dating. He stopped coming out with us, which was fine; some guys aren't players. But every guy needs to be an asset.

## 82. Never Tell Her She's Beautiful

Never tell a woman she is beautiful. Are you kidding me?! You must have rocks in your head if you are considering this. The only time you can say this to a woman is after you have put a ring on her finger. By that time your life is over so it won't matter. Every good-looking woman in this world has had a thousand guys tell her she is beautiful, or stare at her, or whistle at her, etc. Do not be just another guy. A woman understands that the 'beautiful' compliment takes the *least* amount of imagination or thought. To her, you're probably just another horny caveman thinking with your dick.

Furthermore, by telling her she is beautiful you are building her up and ending the challenge right then and there. You need to keep her guessing. Women want a challenge. Talk to her and say some things that will stimulate her. Keep her wondering so she isn't quite sure if you are physically attracted to her or not. Don't be the dumbass with nothing better to say than "You are beautiful."

## 83. Compliments

First of all, don't compliment her that much. It is a sign of weakness and she will get turned off. If you feel the need to give her a compliment, make it an out of the ordinary one. I advise telling a woman she is 'different.' Tell her she is 'down-to-earth'. Tell her she seems like a, 'genuine person, and those are hard to find these days.' You can tell her she seems like a 'free spirit.' Those are the type of compliments she will re-member.

You can also tell her you like her perfume, you like her smile, things of that nature. And of course, you can tell you like her hair. But just keep the compliments to a minimum.

## 84. Flowers

Flowers are a smart move. Buying a girl a bouquet of flowers or a dozen roses is always wise. Surprising her with flow-ers makes a very favorable impression. Flowers go a long way! This gesture has helped me get laid numerous times. Flowers will keep her thinking about you. Showing up for a date with flowers is such an old fashioned thing to do, but chicks really love it. Every time she comes home, she will see or smell the flowers and think of you. Same thing is true if you have flow-ers sent to her at work. She will be surprised and impressed. It will make her look good in front of her co-workers, and she will like you for that. Every time she steps in her office, she will smell the flowers and think of you.

Make giving flowers a part of your monthly routine. You can never go wrong giving a girl flowers.

## 85. No Chocolates

Only a big dummy would buy his girl a box of choco-lates. Are you crazy? Chocolate is extremely fattening. If your girl eats chocolate or craves chocolate often, she will end up being fat. I will never date a girl who munches on chocolate all the time. Don't encourage her. You want to keep your girl in good shape and looking hot for as long as possible. Buy her flowers, or lingerie, or dinner, but not chocolate.

## 86. The Airport Ride

Boy, does this favor go a *long* way. This can't be em-phasized enough. A good way to make a great impression on a girl is to offer to take her to the airport or pick her up from the airport. This can really win a girl over. Most girls who are single don't have anyone to take them to the air-port, or pick them up. They have girlfriends, but girls don't want to bother their friends for a ride when they can easily take a taxi or public transportation. You give her a ride, and she'll think you are special, no doubt. I won't delve into the reasons on this one, just try it and you'll definitely reap the benefits.

I have even used this one on girls I've just met. I'll be at a bar talking to some chick. We'll be hitting it off and I will get her phone number. She will mention how she is flying some-where for business later in the week. I'll say, "Do you need a ride home from the airport on Sunday?" She will contemplate it for a few seconds, and before she responds I'll throw out there, "How 'bout this; I'll pick you up at the airport if you'll agree to have to dinner with me." It is a smooth way to confirm a date. Once on the date, you'll both be more comfortable with each other because of the ride from the airport. The ride from the airport is like a first date. Now you're past the dreaded first date and onto the second date! Even if she says no, she will think you are a nice guy and want to see you again. Airport rides always generate good results.

## 87. Men Age Like Wine

Do not worry about getting older and still trying to pick up women. Men age much more gracefully than women. Almost all women have no problem being with an older man. In fact, in most countries outside of America women prefer older men. I have seen guys in their 40s in Europe and South America with smokin-hot girlfriends in their early 20s. I am perfectly comfortable in my 30s dating chicks in their early 20s. I have predominantly dated women on average ten years younger. I have dated 19 year olds and milfs, cougars, poptarts, and everything in between. Men have the advantage of being able to date women of all ages.

There is an old proverb, "Men age like wine, women age like milk."

Women are much more insecure about the aging process. It starts at 24½ and carries on throughout a woman's entire life. Women hate getting older. Men? Let's face it; men get better as they get older. George Clooney is a pretty old dude. He never got any ass until his hair turned a little snowy. Men get more distinguished looking later in life. An older man is more knowledgeable and experienced. Older men are usually in a better financial position. There are many, many reasons why older men are appealing.

I wish someone would have informed me of this when I was younger. When I was 27 I was dating this hot 20 year old. She was virgin (for a while). I remember thinking that I was close to being too old for this chick. Little did I know! Every year I get older I continue to date girls in their early 20s. We are blessed to be men!

Riki & I have has been on 16 Spring Breaks in a row, a modern day world record. Riki swears that young girls love older guys. Every year we get older but the Spring Break girls stay the same age, and they're always fun to party with.

My buddy Todd lives by the Half Plus Seven Rule. The Half Plus Seven Rule says that your ideal chick should be half your age plus seven. If you are 32, you should be dating a 23 year old (32/2 + 7 = 23).

Never let age become a factor. You're lucky to be a man!

## 88. Appearance

Appearance doesn't matter nearly as much as what comes out of your mouth. However, I see so many knuckle-heads make appearance faux pas that this section had to be included. I don't know if guys are lazy or they just want chicks to accept them for who they are. Then they go home with no pussy and wonder why. Guys who care about their appearance succeed more! This is a fact. Here are some appearance tips.

- Wear one cologne. Rather than using a different cologne every night, use just one. Make it your trademark. The reason is you want women to remember you. You want to develop a memorable scent. This will make her subconsciously remember you. Even better, if you go home with her, her clothes, her sheets, her pillow will smell like your cologne. Every time she smells that cologne she will think of you.

- Expensive jeans. If there is one *must have* item that every man needs in his closet, its one pair of expensive jeans. You can wear a $5 raggedy t-shirt, worn out socks, worn out shoes, and your sweet pair of $100 jeans ~ you'll feel like a million bucks! A money pair of jeans can go anywhere. Dress up, dress down, dress casual, go to a ballgame, anything. You will be in a good mood, you'll feel confident, you'll look great, and chicks will notice.

- No t-shirts underneath the dress shirt. If you wear a dress shirt out at night, please don't wear a t-shirt on underneath it. I see this look all over America. A guy will have a cool dress shirt on, the top two or three buttons undone, and then a t-shirt on underneath. Why?! It's like the t-shirt is his security blanket. This gives off the wrong vibe man. It says to a girl, 'I am a conservative guy; I'm too chicken to wear this dress shirt without a t-shirt.'
Rarely if ever has a guy with a t-shirt on under a dress shirt met a chick and scored that night. The t-shirt ruins the look of the dress shirt and it immediately passes you off as a conservative guy. Chicks go home with confident cool guys, so lose the t-shirt.

- Don't be a suit. Outside of a wedding, guys who wear suits never score with chicks. You see these after-work-guys wearing suits trying to hit on chicks. Yeah sure, you look money in a suit, we all do. But chicks automatically group suits in a different category. Suits remind chicks of their father, or ex-husband, or some conservative guy in their office. You sure as hell aren't going to score with a chick *that night* in a suit, and you will have to work your ass off just to get a phone number. Lose the suit when it's party time.

- No ties. If you are going to formal event like a ritzy party or a buddy's wedding and you are going to wear a suit, I recommend wearing the suit with a dress shirt and *no* tie. This look gets much more attention than the standard suit and tie. The tie makes you look stuffy. The suit with no tie makes you look like you are up for anything.

- Use a tailor. Do you have a shirt in your wardrobe that you love but it doesn't fit right? You wear it out often, but it's just a little too long past your waste? It almost covers your crotch. Or maybe you have a shirt that is pretty cool, but it feels like it was made for a fat guy? Most dress shirts have this problem. Stop being that guy that wears those shirts! This problem is easily solved by a tailor. I see guys at the nightclub and their shirt looks like it was made for a football player. They look ridiculous. Fix it!

It only costs $20 bucks to have a tailor fix it so that the shirt fits perfectly. Pick just one of your favorite shirts and take it to your nearest tailor. Walk in there in tell him that you need your shirt fitted to your body. He will have you try it on, and he will see the problem. He will shorten it, or narrow it, or widen it, or whatever you need. You'll get the shirt back in a week and you'll love it. I now take all my shirts in to my tailor and they fit exactly the way I want them to.

- Wrinkled travel clothes. Anybody who travels knows that it is impossible to keep shirts from getting extremely wrinkled on a road trip. This can ruin your game when you are out at night. I have tried suitcases, garment bags, carry-ons, everything. Shirts still get wrinkled. Bringing a portable iron takes up too much space and having the hotel bring you an iron is a pain in the ass. There is a solution. Turn the shower on in your bathroom as hot as it will go. Hang your shirts in there on a hanger on the shower rod. Close the door and leave. Come back 5–10 minutes later and your shirts are wrinkle-free.

- Trim it. Do you like a chick with a big hairy jungle bush or do you prefer a nice trimmed beaver? Trimmed *of course*. Well, chicks are the same way! They don't want some hairy caveman all over them. They want clean cut.

Trim your hairs. All of them. Don't be the hairy guy. An untrimmed chest or back makes you look old and unconcerned about your appearance. Ever seen Sean Connery as James Bond? There is no need to look like a 1970s playboy with a super hairy chest. Trim your chest hairs and you'll look fit and younger.

If you have a hairy back or hairy shoulders, shave them! Don't think people don't care. That is *not* attractive, and people do notice. Don't be lazy about this. Have your back waxed if you have a hairy back. If you have a unibrow, trim that too.

Finally, the most important place to trim: your crotch. Keep your pubics in check! You love it when a woman has a nice shaved beaver, or even better, a perfect 'landing strip.' Well women prefer a clean cut crotch area for sure. Trim it down there so it is short and manageable. And continue this upkeep as often as needed. Women will definitely appreciate it.

- Not so clean hair. Shampoo companies will have you believe you need to wash your hair every day. Not so. Wash it every third shower. My hair looks best after two days of no shampoo. Washing your hair everyday is just overkill.

- Get the gray out. There are some guys who get gray hair too early in life. Color the gray out of your hair. Why would you not?! It will make you look younger. The process is easy. The results will be drastic.

- Anti-aging cream. This might be a little feminine for some, but a facial cream will do wonders for your long-term looks. There is no reason to look older than you are. There is every reason to try and look as young as possible. The new anti-aging creams that are out there now are amazing. Use of a good cream will prevent wrinkles from appearing much earlier than they normally would, and decrease current wrinkles. (Despite claims, they will not remove wrinkles.) You can begin using an anti-aging cream in your mid to late 20s. I wish I had started then. I am a firm believer in these though. The one I have found to be the best is La Mer Wrinkle Cream from France. I put it on after dinner three times a week. The stuff is expensive but well worth it. I swear by the stuff. This stuff has been instrumental in my ability to still pull hot young poptarts.

- Whiten your teeth. Whitening your teeth can make you look much much better. Nowadays, the process is easy. Your dentist can do it in one day for a few hundred bucks. Or you can order the mouthpiece and bleach stuff online and do it yourself at home. It makes a world of difference. Women find a nice, white set of teeth very attractive! I didn't realize this at first until I noticed my one buddy getting compliment after compliment on his teeth. He said all he did was bleach them. He told me how to buy the stuff online and I did. The first time I did it, I went out with my buddies the very next night. Sure enough, some broad complimented me on my teeth that night. I couldn't believe it. This is a simple and inexpensive process and the results will be significant.

- Eat healthier. Okay, I'm not going to preach to you about health, but I will say that it is in your best interest to eat healthy. It will make you look better physically and it will build your self esteem. Guys who eat healthier do better with women.

I was out of shape for a while. The amount of pussy I got was in sharp decline. I knew something had to be done. I don't have a lot of will power, so I decided to cut out *one* unhealthy thing per month. Billy Conroy's Low-Will-Power Diet:

Month 1 – No more McDonalds. I cut out fast food. This meant no more Mickey Ds, Burger King, Wendys, Jack in the Box, Carls Jr, Taco Bell, etc. Instead, I go to sandwich shops and healthy burrito places. McDonalds is nasty anyway, so this should be the easiest one.

Month 2 – No cheese. Burgers and sandwiches taste just as good without the cheese. Ask for no cheese. Find other spices or condiments you like. Your food will taste just as good without cheese.

Month 3 – Skip the elevator. Use the stairs whenever possible. Park in the farthest parking spot so you can walk more. Exercise.

Month 4 – No mayonnaise. Mayo is pretty damn fattening. Order stuff with no mayo; you won't miss it that much at all. Order honey mustard or relish instead. Buy reduced-fat mayo in the grocery store.

Month 5 – No more soda or pop. This stuff is so bad for you in so many different ways. And it ruins your teeth. Cut out soda and you'll be healthier for sure. This is a big one.

Month 6 – No more french fries. Fried food is packed with fat. Cutting out deep fried food is easy, except for french fries. If you have to have a side dish, order a baked potato or mashed potatoes or a salad. Substitute the french fries.

Month 7 – Drink bottled water all the time. Minimum of two bottles per day. Have water with every meal. Have a bottle of water at your desk and in your car. Water makes you lose weight! Drinking water makes you crave snacks less often. Water makes you full. Water has zero calories. And fresh drinking water tastes great!

Month 8 – No more doughnuts. Every time you want a doughnut, have a banana instead.

Month 9 – Cut out my Four Most Fattening Foods in America. No more biscuits & gravy, no more Bloomin Onion or Cheese Fires at Outback Steakhouse, no more Oreo cookies, and no more Buffalo Wings. Did you know eating one Bloomin Onion is like eating four Big Macs? Buffalo wings are so fattening. Eating just ten will give you 131% of your daily recommended fat intake! You can't eat for the rest of the day if you have 8 Buffalo wings. Same with biscuits and gravy. And Oreo cookies are filled with just awful stuff.

Month 10 – Pizza only once a month. I love it too much to cut it out completely. Having it once a month is a compromise, and it gives me something to look forward too.

Month 11 – Switch to organic milk. Did you know cows are injected with growth hormones? Basically, cows are on steroids. Steroids are very, very bad for your health. They can cause cancer, limp dick, and all kinds of other bad stuff. Pay the extra money for the organic milk. You will thank me later.

Month 12 – No more eating past 9pm. You eat late snacks and then go to bed; that makes you fat. Set a 9pm time limit and stick to it. No munching on cookies, chips, or anything past 9pm. Late night burritos when you are drunk are Okay though, once in a while.

Now you've got a diet that will keep you looking great for years. This diet and regular exercise will add years to your life. After twelve months I looked better, had a lot more energy, and did much better with women. Diet is very important.

# IV. Special Situations

# 89. The Horny Eights Phenomenon

I have to write about this rarely seen phenomenon because when it does happen, it is literally heaven on earth. This phenomenon occurs when there is an over abundance of girls in a bar or nightclub. Not only are there many, many females, there are an over abundance of gorgeous 9s and 10s. Yes, I know, many will shake their head in disbelief, but it does happen, and I have witnessed this rare and exciting phenomenon.

On a normal night, you might run into one chick who is just off-the-charts smoking hot. She will be the one everyone is staring at. Categorically, she'll be a 9 or 10. She'll know she is the queen of the club. Then there will be a few 8s and 7s sprinkled around. The 8s and 7s are use to getting all the attention and being the most sought after. A chick who is an 8 in my book is pretty damn hot. Because there are so few 9s and 10s, the 8s are accustomed to running the show and getting any guy they want. Then there are plenty of 5s and 6s and they are the easiest ones to score with. 3s and 4s usually don't come out, nor should they.

Well, every couple years or so the planets align and for some strange reason all the smoking hot chicks end up going out on the same night to the same place. Imagine walking into some club or party and seeing all 9s and 10s. You would flip out! It's a sight to be seen.

An amazing thing occurs when there are 9s and 10s everywhere. The 8s begin to feel ignored, and that leads to a heightened level of insecurity. They are not use to feeling like second-rate citizens. It is a feeling they are not accustomed to, and they react like a caged tiger. They become competitive. They actually become the aggressor and they crave attention. They want to hook up in order to feel desired. All of the

7s and 8s become very slutty when they are surrounded by 9s and 10s.

During this phenomenon, 8s are *ready to go* with little or no work. They might even approach you! Or wink at you...or stare at you....or smile at you. I know, I know! This never happens. But it does when there's a Horny Eights Phenomenon occurring, and I've seen it.

I've witnessed it exactly seven times so far in my life (I go out a lot.) I saw it once at a nightclub in San Diego in the late 90s, a couple times in LA, once at a fancy nightclub in Brazil, once in Chicago at Le Passage in 2003, once in Vegas at a private party, and a couple times in Miami in 2002 and 2007. Each of those were incredible nights. All seven nights were very memorable. People say they remember where they were when we landed on the moon or when the Twin Towers went down. I remember where I was when the Horny Eights Phenomenon occurred.

Each of those nights, every guy I was with, including myself, went home with hot chicks. All seven times the venue was packed wall-to-wall with women. Probably 70% women, no exaggeration. 9s and 10s and models and strippers *everywhere*! I'm getting horny now just reminiscing. A bar with 50% women feels like 75%. So imagine a place with 70% women. It feels like 90%! Seeing smoking hot 9s and 10s walk around a place is enough to make you lose your cool. Many guys do. The important thing is to remain calm and remember your goal. Your goal is to get laid *that night* or in the very near future. But don't be too calm and relax by the bar and gaze in astonishment at all the hot women you are surrounded by. You need to get in there and mix it up. You need to start talking to women. If you wait too long the ratio could get ruined by vultures showing up or hot chicks leaving because there aren't enough men to satisfy their need for attention.

I can tell a good getting-laid story from just about every one of those nights. I will just tell one - it happened in LA. We had some buddies living in LA. I was living in San Diego at the time. A few of us drove up from San Diego, and a few more were in Cali on vacation. There were 12 of us going out that night. If you know anything about LA, there is no way in hell twelve dudes are getting in anywhere. Especially not the hottest nightclub in town at the time, The Garden Of Eden. We had no 'juice' there at all, so it was going to be tough to just get two guys in, let alone 12. We decided to go very early (around 9pm, which is unheard of in LA.) We decided to go in groups of three. I was in the first group.

At 9pm we were parking. There was already a growing line to get in, and it was mostly chicks. Hot chicks. Riki bullshitted with the doorman and got us in by 9:30pm.

We walked in and the place was already pretty crowded. Apparently, everyone had a tough time getting in to Garden Of Eden so many people go early. We made our way to the bar. Our heads were on a swivel. It was *all* chicks, and they were *all* smoking hot. Because of the nature of the city, LA chicks might be the hottest in the world. These chicks were all dressed in short skirts or some sexy outfit. Cleavage everywhere. And I'm telling you the place was all hot, hot, hot girls! It was fucking paradise. Dabert, Riki and I were in a state of shock. Dabert said, "Oofah, there are *a lot* of hot chicks here." I said, "Holy crap, what is going on?!" Riki said, "All of these chicks are thirsty for cock! Yeah! Let's party!"

We ordered some drinks and turned to take in this amazing spectacle. Right after I got my drink I saw this chick a few feet away looking at me. Dabert, Riki, and I were still grabbing each other saying, 'Oh my god, oh my god!' under our breath, so I didn't really pay attention to the eye-contact from the girl. Next thing I know she was up next to me trying to order a drink. I wasn't planning on talking to her but I said, "You look thirsty." Nothing special, just something to say. Remember, saying *something* is always better than saying nothing.

She turned to me and said something and grabbed my wrist briefly to emphasize her point. It was on. This chick was probably an 8, maybe a 7.5. However, there were at least 50 girls there hotter than she was. Normally, I would be thrilled to hook up with a hot chick like her, but when there are that many chicks better looking than she was, I wasn't that thrilled.

Note: Deciding whether to trade-up or not is a difficult decision. Do you stay with the sure thing or try to trade up for a better looking girl? If you are in with a 7 and you know you can take her home, why not try for a 9? Aaahhh, this is a dilemma for all mankind. Many young bucks dump the 7, try for the 9, and wind up with nothing. Then they get desperate late night and go home with a 4. Not good! On the flip side, the guy who stays with the 7 regrets it in the morning. He says to himself, "My game was on fire last night. Why did I settle for this chick?!" The moral: The grass is always greener bro. Whatever decision you make, be happy with it. I usually try to trade up. But I hold my 7 for as long as possible. I make frequent trips to the bar and to the bathroom trying to meet a hotter girl. If I don't, the 7 is usually still there waiting for me.

On this night, I decided to stay with my 8 and figure the rest out later. I took her over to the nearest place to sit. It was some S-shaped sofa right near the front bar. It didn't take long before we were making out. We talked for a little while. She had a friend there but couldn't find her and wasn't concerned about finding her. (It's amazing how a little attention can replace a girl's need to remain with her friend).

The place began to really fill up. This girl was on me like stink on shit....and I was enjoying every minute of it. She was asking me about my job and how I got into the business. I had told her I was a stuntman, so now I had to answer all these stuntman questions. I tried to stop the questions by kissing more. The making out was going well. I could tell she was a horny girl. I decided to put her left hand on my package. She started rubbing it, and I knew that was a good sign.

*Point of Advice: One of the best indicators to find out if you are going to score or not is to put your chick's hand directly on your crotch. If she pulls away immediately in shock, you are not getting laid. If she starts rubbing it like a magic lamp waiting for the genie to pop out, you are getting laid. If she kind of pulls away and smiles and gently says, "No, not now," you are getting a blowjob, or maybe laid.*

So this girl was rubbing my package and we were making out. I always like to push the envelope when things are going well, so I unzipped my pants and pulled my hog out. I held my shirt over it so you couldn't really see it. She put her hand under my shirt and on my hog. She kept it there. I was pretty happy about that. Riki and Dabert could see me, they were smiling, but they had other priorities. They were still mesmerized by all the hot girls there. I kissed my girl some more and noticed some of our other friends showing up coming through the front door.

Meanwhile, my girl hated it when I would look away. She was into me and wanted all my attention. The Horny Eights Phenomenon was in full effect, and she must have been worried I would see a hotter girl and leave her.

I kissed her some more and now she was full-on stroking my hog out in the open for the whole world to see. I didn't care. She looked like a mushroom farmer. We were sitting down, but there were no tables, so anybody could see it if they just looked down. It was dark in there and everyone was standing up so we thought we were shielded. She was kissing on my neck and stroking my hard cock when I noticed all eleven of my friends were peeking over shoulders watching me. It was 10pm and they had all just arrived and were grouping by the bar. They were amazed that not only had I hooked up already, but that she was giving me a hand job right there in the front bar. I could see some of my buddies cracking up looking at me. And I could see a few of the dudes that were friends of friends with their mouths wide open, astounded because they'd never seen a hand job in public before.

She stroked it some more but I ended up putting it back in my pants. I was worried about getting kicked out for indecent exposure. We hung out there for another hour, but it seemed like three hours. I had a tough decision to make. Take her out of there and miss the rest of an incredible night. Or leave a for-sure piece of ass and go party with my friends and try to trade up. A dilemma for the ages.

Remember #46. Always bang first. She was a little drunk and wanted to leave. I got Dabert's car keys and took her out of there. She was parked in the same parking garage. Dabert had a SUV with tinted windows. She and I got in his backseat. It didn't take long before we were banging. The sex was good, not great. Banging in the backseat is never ideal. I wasn't hammered though, like I normally am, so I enjoyed it a lot more. She was happy too.

Afterwards she wanted me to come home with her and hang out all night. Another dilemma for the ages. How do I get out of this? Everything I have said up until now has been along the lines of, 'I like you and I want to spend time with you.' Now I need to get away without hurting her feelings. I told her that I can't leave because all of my friends were inside. That wasn't enough. I told her that this was a one friend's birthday night and it would be wrong of me to leave. That wasn't enough. I told her that I would call her first thing in the morning and promised her we would hang out all day tomorrow. That was barely enough. I walked her to her car. She gave me a big kiss goodbye and went home. She called me as soon as she got home and left a message saying she had a great time. Meanwhile, I had to go fight my way back in the club. The line was huge and I was solo. I gave the doorman all the money I had left (maybe $45 bucks) and he let me back in for round two.

I found my crew. We were all cracking up and they were telling me how everyone in the club was watching me get a handjob. Then we all focused and tried to get some chicks.... which we did. I was in a really good mood because I'd already gotten laid, so I was on fire. I met this really hot brunette with gorgeous green eyes. She was a solid 9. Maybe a 9.5. Yeah, that hot. Talked her up for while. She had to leave though because her girlfriend was leaving. Got her digits. Then met a really hot blond beach girl. She was an 8. Great natural boobs. Her and I were talking and teasing each other. The conversations was heating up. We were talking about sex and favorite positions and all kinds of kinky shit.

We had a big afterparty back at Grady's house and partied till the sun came up. I boned the beach girl in Grady's bed. She was an All-Star in bed. Great sex.

I actually dated the brunette with green eyes for a couple months. She was hot and cool. I liked her a lot and was bummed when it ended. She is going to be pissed after reading this and discovering that I banged two chicks the night I met her. Oh well, it was a Horny Eights Phenomenon.

## 90. The Four Cardinal Rules of A Gangbang

Four mandatory gangbang rules have been passed down by our fore-fathers. These rules are set in stone, and now I will pass them on to you.

**#1. No laughing.** Only a very inexperienced gangbang guy would attempt to break this rule. There is no laughing because, first of all, it can make the girl feel uncomfortable. Second, it can completely ruin a guy's concentration.

I was out in Boulder, CO for a wedding, hanging out at a bar. My buddy Hoss leaned over the table and asked me, "Bill, how is it I always hear all these threesome and gangbang stories from you? How do you do it? I could never find girls that are into that?"

But he was wrong. Sexually adventurous women live and work among us. You just have to know what to look for.

I said "Hoss, you just have to be able to spot them bro." I motioned to the cute inebriated college girl to his left. No way, he said. He knew her.

"That girl is *down* for a gangbang dude!" I said quietly.

This girl had all the tell-tale signs of a girl down for a wild night. She had already done a few shots. She wasn't getting all the attention she wanted. Her clothes were slightly more provocative than the average hippy, tree-hugger chick in that Colorado bar. Every so often she would throw puppy-dog-eyes at my buddy Hoss. She had a trampstamp tattoo above her ass. She had recently broken up with her boyfriend, and she needed a ride home. She basically had a neon sign above her head that said, "Gangbang Potential, Tonight Only, Inquire Within."

Hoss didn't believe it, but I convinced him to invite Denise (let's call her Denise) back with us.

During the car ride home I physically had to push Hoss' hand over so he would start rubbing Denise's leg. She was fine with that, of course. If she would have removed his hand or acted cold, gangbang was off. But she didn't. I instructed Hoss to get her straight to the bedroom when we got home, thereby avoiding the living room and all the dull stories and get-to-know-you crap that might stall all festivities.

Next thing you know we were all in the bedroom; they were on the bed. I threw on some music, *Last Night* by P Diddy, medium volume. I quietly closed the door, dimmed the lights, and pre-opened some condoms. I know how to orchestrate a gangbang bro. I got buck naked so that Denise felt more comfortable taking off some of her own clothes. She was making out with Hoss. I began kissing her neck so she knew I was there. I pulled her over and she started making out with me. Hoss inched down past her belly, peeled off her jeans and started munching her box.

It turned out to be the only competent thing he did that night.

She arched her back like she was enjoying it. I knew it was time to party.

I scooted up and, and with a little encouragement, she started sucking on my schlong. I was going up and down while straddling her as she was blowing me. I pulled out and tea-bagged her for a minute and then put my cock back in her mouth. I like tea-bagging. She continued sucking it and we were having a good ole time.

I slid down in between her and began squeezing into the length of a condom. For some reason, this sparked Hoss giggling like a little schoolgirl.

"Knock it off!" I hissed.

That was my downfall. It can happen that quickly. The combination of alcohol, the damn constricting condom, but mainly his fricken giggling made me lose it down to about 25% hardness. So here I am 25% hard with a condom on, trying to put it in Denise so we can have sex. Talk about frustrating – it just wouldn't work. Denise was drunk, but even she could tell the difference between a pipe and a wet noodle. She was expecting to get laid, and not getting what she wanted.

With a little shame, I bowed out and made room for Hoss. But that bastard couldn't get it up either because he was laughing under his breath. So nobody got to service this poor, horny, tipsy poptart. She had to leave later so that was it. Terrible story, I know. Rule #1 is no laughing.

**#2. No touching.** Right along the lines of Rule #1, there are no high fives, no low fives, no pats on the back. That never helps and it can only ruin concentration. If you are a high-five guy, save that shit for Monday Night Football.

Now if you are in a tag-team and waiting patiently on the sidelines for your buddy to finish, he can motion you in, but never 'tag' you in like a wrestling match. No touching is the rule.

If you have to touch due to the sexual position you are in, that can be tolerated, but no other guy touching is allowed. (Side note - if it is you and two girls, touching is, of course, okay, but that is a threesome, not a gangbang.)

**#3. No eye contact.** No reason to make eye contact with the other guy involved. Most guys can't handle doing anything sexual with another guy in the room. Some of us can. Listen, don't think for an instant that some dude is going to lose his masculinity and throw puppy-dog-eyes at you. He has the same thing on his mind as you; he is enjoying getting laid with this girl. Go about your business with your head down and concentrating on this hot chick.

**#4. No cumming inside her.** This should be the most obvious rule. There is a high probability that someone will be going after you go, so don't mess up everything by blowing your load inside her.

I wasn't there for this one, but I heard all about the next day from Riki and a couple weeks later from Todd.

Riki had found this really hot redhead from LA and she was down for all kinds of things; gangbangs, anal, anything. The great part was that she had a good job and looked like a normal citizen when you saw her. Nobody could tell she was a *faaa-reak* in the sheets. She was in her mid 20s, had a cute face, pale white skin, a great ass, brand new C-cup boobs. She had some 'mystery bruises' all over her legs, but nobody's perfect.

Riki and Todd were in LA one weekend and they ended up at her house late-night. She had this one bedroom vintage apartment off Sunset Blvd. Todd lived in Newport Beach, so anytime we wanted to party in L.A., we'd call Todd and tell him we were coming up from San Diego. Orange County nightlife sucked, so we would always head for L.A.

So Riki and Todd showed up around 5am at Red's house (we'll call her Red.) She must have known what was on their mind showing up at that hour. One thing led to another, and she started going down on Riki.

Riki: Understand that Riki is the Grand Master General of all gangbangs. He excels in this environment. He makes me look like a boy scout. The difference between him & I is that I fall into gangbangs, he actively seeks them out. Riki is stocky and cocky. He's a Hawaiian guy with big muscles, a mischievous demeanor, and a hilarious personality. His idols are Rocco Siffredi and Don Ho. Riki is definitely the shadiest guy I know, and a very fun guy to party with. Riki once dumped a girlfriend when he found out her parents were still married. He says he only dates girls that come from broken homes.

If you party with him at all, at some point in the night you will no doubt hear him say, "Yeaahhhh, these chicks are thirsty for cock. Let's get shady tonight. Owwwww!"

So this chick Red was sucking on Riki's pineapple. Todd was hoping to get involved because Red had such a hot body. Riki was the puppeteer though, so Todd had to be patient.

Riki instructed Red to start going down on Todd. Without hesitation she rolled to her other side and mouthed Todd's cock. Todd was stoked!

Riki then began to remove Red's clothing. Todd hasn't been in nearly as many threesomes or gangbangs as Riki, but he is experienced and does know what he is doing. Riki removed her clothes. Todd continued to enjoy his blowjob.

While she was going down on Todd, Riki began nailing her from behind on the bed. Commence the gangbang!

Todd and Riki moved around the bed like two seasoned gangbang veterans. Everything was going pretty well. Everybody was getting into it.

After a while Todd ended up under her, feet hanging off the bed. She was facing down. Riki was getting her from behind. In the back door. They were DPing her (double penetration.) This chick loved sex and the only words she spoke the entire time were, "Yes, yes, yes," and an "Ooommph," when Riki was slipping it her ass. It was Todd's first DP so he was kind of stoked and kind of tripping out at what a crazy experience it was. Todd was wearing protection, Riki wasn't.

After a good amount of time, Riki starts getting into it. He starts pumping her like a jack-hammer. Todd was properly concentrating on the girl, but he was obviously aware that Riki was jack-hammering her. Riki let out a couple short moans. He was getting close to finishing. Todd must have realized Riki's impending orgasm.

At the last second Todd let out, "Don't cum inside her dude!"

Riki was almost incoherent, but he knew in the back of his mind that he should probably pull out. But he didn't want to. But he had to. So he pulled out at the very, very last second and accidentally came all over Todd's balls. And a little on Todd's shaft and little on Todd's stomach. Riki's head was rolled back and he just kept cumming and cumming.

Todd didn't immediately realize what was happening. But he must have felt it, and then he saw Riki's face look down at that mess. Riki got the expression of like, "Ohhh. Oops. Yuck." Todd saw the grossed out expression on Riki's face. Riki walked away into the bathroom to clean himself up.

Then Todd knew what had happened. What could he do though? This chick was still riding him.

Todd tried to keep going but lost his erection because he kept thinking about the big mess all over down below. Who can perform after that?

That was the end of that gangbang. Todd was pretty perturbed and didn't speak to Riki for a few weeks.

First of all, cumming on your bros balls is a true violation of bro etiquette. Second, yes, Riki upheld gangbang rule

#4, but it is his responsibility to shoot somewhere safe, not on your bro.

Riki apologized later and they patched things up a few weeks later.

## 91. Coercing Her Into A Gangbang

If I saw, "Coercing a girl into a gangbang," in a book, I would think, "Oh yeah, tell me how! I want to have a gangbang tonight!" I wish it were that easy. Fact is gangbangs and threesomes rarely happen. You never know when or how one will happen. They only thing you can do to increase your probability of having one is by going out often and chasing a lot of women.

Surprisingly, many girls are open to having multiple partners if it is under the right circumstances. Rocker Ted Nugent once said, "Every girl has one year in her life where she just goes crazy wild." If you find a girl in her wild, slutty stage, anything can happen. Of course, it helps if she is intoxicated and really horny.

If the potential gangbang is two or more guys and one girl, one of the guys needs to take the lead and be the guy to do all the talking. Similar to good cop, bad cop, but instead it is coercive cop and quiet, confirming cop. What the coercive cop says is vital to the gangbang. Saying the wrong thing can make the girl feel slutty and cheap. Saying too little or nothing at all will not inspire the girl to partake in such an adventurous sexual act. She will obviously be somewhat hesitant to take on two guys, so I always say, "Wow, you are so lucky; this is a girl's fantasy." She knows two girls and one guy is a guy's fantasy.

Why can't the opposite be true as well? I will continue, "You're so lucky to be spoiled by two good guys." These are both stellar things to say, and they will set the tone for her to enjoy the experience. If she remains hesitant so you can always throw in, "It's good to try everything once, right?" And then I continue to reinforce the first two points, repeating, "You are so lucky. Let us spoil you."

The second guy needs to be there to confirm what the 1st guy is saying. Back him up. Agree with everything the first guy is saying, rub her leg and stuff like that. Don't seem overly eager. Just act like you also want to try something new.

She definitely needs positive reinforcement from both guys. As you can see, the emphasis needs to be on *her* experience, not your experience. If you say something like "Come on, please let us have sex with you," you will never get anywhere.

One last bit of advice. Take chances. If you are partying with some girl and you think she might be a willing participant in a gangbang, go for it. Try to kiss her. Take her into the bedroom. Don't be shy. Take a chance. Worse thing that can happen is she says no. I have seen many guys hooked up with gullible, horny chicks yet they won't lean over and kiss her or take her in the back bedroom. Take chances. That's the only way these things happen.

## 92. Coercing Two Girls Into A Threesome

The unfortunate truth about coercing two girls into having sex with you is that it is nearly impossible. Women will easily be with two guys they don't know, but not some girl they don't know. And the reason is simple. Women prefer the penis.

Many girls will kiss other girls, but that is just for show. To get two women to sleep with you, the circumstances have to be absolutely perfect. Both girls usually have to be friends, but not too good of friends. Otherwise, they will be uncomfortable and each girl will be too timid to make the first move. Aside from them being friends, the only other thing I can recommend is not blowing it verbally. If you say bluntly, "Let's have a threesome?" odds are you will not. Most threesomes with two women just gradually happen with no words being spoken. The way to coerce is though gestures, body movement, and physical contact. Drop hints about a threesome. Once both girls understand what you are proposing and you see that they are not opposed to the idea, then you can be more explicit about your intentions.

I brought back this college girl from a bar in Manhattan Beach, California. She was really tall, maybe 5'9 or 5'10, light brunette hair, great ass, which is rare for a tall chick, no boobs, tan and drunk. She was living in Arizona attending U. of A. at the time. She was visiting her girlfriend. After the bar closed we headed to her friend's house on the beach. When we arrived at her friend's house I was still wondering whether or not I was going to get any action. She made out with me and then left me on the couch. I was like, 'What the hell?' Five or ten minutes went by so I decided to go find this girl. I don't know why I waited! I went into the only bedroom and there she was in bed with her girlfriend. They both stopped talking and smiled at me. I jumped right in the middle of them. The girl's friend, the one who lived there, was *hot*, even hotter than my chick, but in a more innocent, cute kind of way. She had short blond hair, a tight little tan rocket body and a hot face. She looked like a sexy schoolgirl.

Small talk happened for a couple minutes and then I started making out with the girl I met at the bar. Things were going well and I got myself and her naked. We were under the covers and I tried slipping it in her. She said no. I kept trying and she kept saying, "Mmmm no," three or four times. The other girl, who was wearing panties and nothing else, surprisingly said, "I want to watch you two have sex." This was exactly what I needed, a good wing-girl. Two more tries and I was in there, all the way, and she was loving it. I was loving it. The friend was getting into it too! It was so good I had to slow down because I didn't want to bust an early nut.

I reached over and started playing with the second girl's nice little firm tits. She was fine with that. I was banging away. I wanted to involve the 2nd girl, so I grabbed her hand and put it on my back hoping she would respond favorably. She got up on her knees and started rubbing my back. Cool.

I leaned over and start making out with her. Very cool. I was totally surprised that she was into this; I figured her for a prissy goody-two-shoes girl. As I was making out with her she slid her hand down my back and started massaging my balls! I almost lost it and blew my load right there! I stopped kissing her but kept banging away. Then I started really banging and moaning. I was about to cum.

I pulled out just in time. The 2nd girl grabs my cock and starts stroking it at the perfect moment. It felt incredible. She had her left hand on my nuts, and her right hand on my cock. A double reach-around! I spooged all over the first girl's stomach. It was a long-lasting incredible orgasm. I thought I had none left at one point and she stroked some more cum out of there somehow. What a champion wing-girl! The first girl was happy to see me cum all over her stomach. I grabbed a towel and cleaned us up. It was a super little threesome.

So, as you can see, there isn't much you can say with two chicks, you kind of just need to let things happen and take advantage of the opportunity. I took a chance by grabbing the other girl while I was having sex with the first girl. That move could have backfired, but as it turns out, was the right thing to do.

I passed out in between the two girls. I remember waking up in the middle of the night and trying to bang the 2nd chick. I really liked her. But she was having none of that.

I woke up in the morning way too early. I smelled pancakes. The 2nd girl was making breakfast; the 1st girl was in the shower. What time was it?! It was like 8:30am on Sunday and these chicks were up and about. What the heck was going on? After a Saturday night of boozing and banging I like to sleep the fuck in. Oh well. I got up and the blond was all perky and happy making breakfast. I went in there wearing only my boxers and my gigolo necklace. I needed some OJ.

She said good morning and then kind of pulled me aside. She said "Billy, could you do me a favor? My boyfriend is coming over to take us to church, so could you put your clothes on and get dressed." She looked at me in a way. I translated what she was saying to, "Please put your clothes on and don't let my boyfriend know that I was stroking your hog last night as you dropped a big yogurt load on my girlfriend."

I complied. I got dressed.

Sure enough, the guy shows up. He was dressed in nice pressed cotton khaki pants, white shirt, navy blue blazer, and a blue tie. He was a good looking young man. He was clean shaven. He had rosy cheeks like he just ran a 5k marathon. His hair was combed to the side neatly. He was a decent looking dude, but just kind of square.

He saw me sitting at the kitchen table going through my phone. I was wearing a black button down dress shirt with a wide collar, wife beater, dark blue designer jeans, black dress boots that zippered up to my lower shin, and a black Gucci belt. My top three or four buttons of my shirt were not buttoned because I was hungover and didn't give a shit. I had an Egyptian cross necklace on that came down to the middle of my chest. My shirt was not tucked in. I had a large expensive silver square watch on. I threw a bunch of water on my face and hair to wake up, so my hair was now wet and completely slicked back. My face was puffy from waking up so early. I could feel the dried cum on my belly that needed to be washed off. And I had cotton mouth in the worst way.

Church started at 10am, and they had to drop me off first, so we had to get going. We can't be late because it turns out the guy that just showed up is the preacher's son, and the father will be giving the sermon today. That was one bizarre car ride home. In the front seat were the two chicks in their best church dresses. We had done some naughty things just five hours earlier, now they were completely different chicks. In the backseat it was me and the well dressed preacher's kid. I remember looking at him and him looking me. You could not have put two opposite guys next to each other. We hadn't had an opportunity to meet so when we looked at each other, there was awkward silence. He then said, "How are you," in a deep voice. I responded, "Good man. How's it going?" No other words were spoken the entire ride. I felt like a villain.

The girls didn't say anything either. They must have been cringing hoping him and I didn't start up a conversation that would have surely began with, "So what did you guys do last night," and I would have surely said, "Orgy, with those two girls." They dropped me off and went to church, but like I said, that car ride was very memorable.

## 93. Get Her Friend Involved

Anytime you are dating a chick, and it is not serious, try to get her girlfriend involved - try for the threesome. Most girls will say no. Some will say, 'maybe.' Very few will say, "No, and I don't want to see you again." So the risk is worth the reward!

One of the best times to shoot for the threesome is when she has a girlfriend visiting from out of town. Set it up so all three of you will meet up that night. Early in the night, pull your girl aside and tell her that you think her friend is hot. Say it as a compliment though, not as a perverted thing. Do your best to get both of them drunk. As the night goes on, find the right time and dare them to kiss each other. This will break the ice. Most of the time they will giggle and politely refuse. If they flatly refuse and are grossed out, it's not gonna happen. But if they kiss, all innocent and cute, it could be on. If they kiss all slutty with tongue, it's definitely on.

Next, present the threesome idea to your chick, without her friend hearing. Asking both of them out of the blue is too abrasive. They will say no, even if they want to. Maybe whisper to your chick, "You know what my fantasy is baby? We should try a threesome sometime." (Throw in the "sometime" just in case she freaks out. You can defend yourself by saying, "I didn't mean now! Geez!")

Once home, pour some wine for everybody, and head for the bedroom. Your chick will follow. Tell her to tell her friend to come drink with you. She will call to her girlfriend to come drink with you two. Then you dim the lights. The friend comes and hangs out on the bed. You put on some cool soul music. You start kissing your girl. You motion for the other girl to come closer. She does. And hopefully it's on....

Couple years ago I was dating this tiny little 19 year old hot freckle-face blond poptart. She was a straight-laced college girl. It took me forever for me to tap that ass the first time. She just wasn't a sexual girl. However, she was hot and young so I kept her on my tip.

Well, one night she had a friend in town from Milwaukee. She called me up and wanted to meet up and party. Both girls had fake IDs to get in bars. I didn't need a fake ID since I was in my 30s (She thought I was 27.)

*Point of Advice: Young chicks cannot tell the difference between 27 and 40. They just know you are older than they are and younger than their parents. You are simply an 'older guy.' Statistically, 1 in 3 poptarts like older men.*

We met up, had some drinks and laughs, and end up back at my townhouse. I put on some on Mary J Blige. The chicks opened a bottle of wine and spilled it all over my nice kitchen. Damn chicks. Fucking red wine everywhere. I remember saying to myself, "Fuckit. I am partying with two hot teenagers!"

I started to think maybe I could somehow score with both of them. We stayed up till 4am though, drinking and just having fun partying. All three of us ended up in my bed. But nothing happened because we were all too shitfaced. I passed out without doing anything.

Middle of the night, my chick starts making out with me. She was a great kisser. I got a rock solid boner. She started tugging on it. Next thing I now, my boxers are off and she scoots on top on me and starts riding me!

She had the tightest little pussy – it was so awesome.

Her friend woke up to us getting it on right next to her. My chick started grabbing and playing with her girlfriend's hair. I took that as my queue to get her involved. I grabbed her and started making out with her while my little spinner girl continued to ride me. If my chick wasn't drunk and wasn't totally enjoying my cock, she would have freaked out for sure. But she didn't. She was having too good of a time, so she went with it. Her friend was taller, brunette, fit, and pretty hot. She looked like a young Daisy Duke. I took her top off, leaving her in nothing but soft pink cotton panties. I don't know why I hadn't noticed before, but this chick had these incredible, bodacious, huge, Wisconsin milk-fed perfect tits. Man, they were nice boobs. I started playing with those things and smacking them together and making out with both girls. It was on! My girl let her guard down and turned into a different person. She started making out with her friend. She was totally into everything that was happening. (I think college girls want to experience everything once.) At one point I was pounding her friend from behind while they were making out passionately. It was fucking magnificent. I considered myself a lucky man after that night. Did them both and had one heck of a great threesome.

Oh yeah, the next morning. I had my townhouse up for sale, and I completely forgot about a 10am showing by a Realtor. At 10am sharp my cell phone was going off. I could barely function to open my eyes and focus, let alone answer the damn phone. I answered it with a cackle, "Huu-llo." The guy calling says, in a perky annoying voice, "Hi Mr. Conroy this is James with Markham Realty. We are here for our 10am appointment."

I snarl, "Well come back at 10am then."

He says, "Mr. Conroy, it is ten after ten and we are pressed for time." I say, "Uh, Oh, okay, I'll come let you in." Five or so minutes later I let them in.

The Realtor and this well-dressed yuppie couple in their 40s come in. I was wearing a wife-beater and basketball shorts. My hair was sticking straight up. I looked completely disheveled, and the place smelled like cheap Merlot. I said right off, "Listen, I have to be honest, I forgot about this appointment so I apologize. The place isn't very clean; do you still want to see it?" They said yes.

I showed them the kitchen, and the living room, the balcony, the 2nd bedroom. Of course they wanted to see the master bedroom and master bath. So all four of us walk in there. The blinds were shut, but there was still plenty of daylight. There were two 19-year-old chicks wearing nothing but sexy panties passed out face down in my bed. The comforter was off to the side so you could pretty much see everything. These people were kind of mortified. They tried to contain themselves. The wife stopped and the husband bumped into her. Man, I'll never forget the looks on their faces as they were trying to figure out everything. The Realtor was shocked too. His eyes almost popped out of his head. He was cool though. He kept looking over at me like I was tha man. They all quickly peeked at the master bathroom and went back through the bedroom to the kitchen, and eventually left. I turned on some football and ordered a pizza.

The chicks, being college chicks, didn't get up until 1pm. We were all hanging out and they were cleaning my kitchen and I told them that very story. They didn't believe it at first, that people had walked through the bedroom, but I assured them it was true. They thought it was the funniest story. We laughed about it for a while. They left a couple hours later. It was a great time no doubt.

## 94. Strippers Love To Party

Strippers are a whole different breed. Strippers just love to party. Anytime you meet a stripper, it is your duty to hit on her and try to hook up with right then and there. I don't go to titty bars that often, but every time I do, I am trying to pull a stripper out of there. I'm not stuffing $20s down her bra, I am doing everything in my power to coerce her to come meet me later at the nightclub. I put on the full-court press to get her out of there. With a little persuasion, a little alcohol, and a couple witty comments, usually they are ready to go.

Throwing a bunch of money at strippers will get classified as a meal-ticket instead of a cool dude they want to hang out with. That's why I like to separate myself from the customers.

I have pulled many a stripper out of stripclubs in Vegas. Chicks love to party with fun guys. Some of time they want drugs and I don't have any, but usually they just want to hang out with outgoing guys, party, laugh, and suck cock. That's why I love strippers!

You can say anything to strippers. They like guys who get down and dirty. They like guys who treat them like a party buddy. They don't like nice guy, straight laced shmucks. So be different. Be forward. Be confident and be fun. You'll be on your way to scoring with strippers.

Don't know why, but every time I talk about strippers, it always reminds me of this stripper my buddy VJ was dating.

VJ was a pretty crazy guy who wasn't shy about anything. VJ was a decent looking guy. He was not tall, he had big muscles from taking too much HGH, brown hair, big fish lips, and hair parted to the side with bangs that need to be cut or slicked back, but weren't.

One time a couple chicks we knew, who were neighbors with VJ, accidentally walked in on him beating off. He was on the couch watching a porno stroking it. The door was wide open on sunny day so they just walked right in. These chicks told us about it that night. Apparently, VJ saw them out of the corner of his eye, but never turned his head. He snarled at them, "Get out of here," never stopped beating off, and kept his eyes fixated on the TV.

The girls were taken aback. They just turned and walked out. That's what kind of guy VJ was.

So anyway, VJ was dating this stripper on the side. She wasn't his main chick, but he nailed her every so often. We always asked about her, hoping to hook up with her hot stripper friends. One night a bunch of us were pre-partying before we went out, listening to some Red Hot Chillipeppers and drinking beer. I asked VJ if he was still seeing that stripper. He said, "Kind of." Then he casually started telling us how he was boning her the night before.

They just got back from a big steak dinner. He said he was doing her from behind, doggystyle, and low and behold he looks down and sees a big brown terd starting to come out of her poopshoot. WTF!

"Peeking out like a shy little turtle," was how he put it.

We were all like, "Whoaaaa?! That's nasty dude!"

I thought that was it so we kept on drinking. Then one guy said, "What did you do? Stop?" VJ looked at him with an expression of, 'Are you crazy dumbass?' VJ said, "No dude." Then VJ licked his thumb and said, "I just pushed it back in and kept going until I finished." He showed us how he used his thumb to push it back in.

I spit my beer out when I saw that.

We were all a little grossed out, but that was VJ, so we understood. One guy told him he should have given her a Dirty Sanchez, but VJ said "No, that's gross. I just wanted to get my nut."

Like I said, strippers are down for anything. Never be shy around a stripper.

## 95. Large Bachelorette Parties

If you are out on the town often, it is inevitable you'll spot a number of bachelorette parties. Don't get overly excited. A lot of the time bachelorette parties are full of girls who are married or engaged or fat or bitchy, etc. Much will depend on what type of bachelorette party it is. There are many types.

If it's a fat-chick bachelorette party, they will probably harass you and ask you to pin condoms on the girl's t-shirt and crap like that. Stay away from fat-chick bachelorette parties.

Also, stay away from small bachelorette parties where it's only four or five girls. Small bachelorette parties are a waste of time. Their only concern is *being there* for the bachelorette. They will not hook up with guys because that might piss off the bachelorette by taking attention away from her. They usually cling to the bride-to-be and won't talk to anyone unless she is involved in the conversation. They are insecure and boring.

Large bachelorette parties are a completely different story. A large group of girls together like that can get worked up in a frenzy and the only thing that can cure that euphoria is cock. A large group of girls can invoke competition. This makes girls easy to hit on and easy to hook up with. Often times there will be so many girls in a large bachelorette party that some will get starved for attention and just want to meet a man.

Furthermore, with so many girls, there will be some who don't know the bride very well. Those girls are probably not having that good of a time and they are prime candidates to be swooped on. They probably feel a little awkward not being in the inner-circle of the bachelorette's friends. They will love the attention you are giving them. They don't know the inner-circle girls that well, so they can be as naughty as they want.

In-town bachelorette parties are always much more tame than out-of-town bachelorette parties. If chicks are on a road-trip away from home on a bachelorette party, throw all the rules out of the window. Anything goes. All girls will be looking for cock, sometimes even the bachelorette herself. (Hey, I've seen it) Bachelorette parties in Las Vegas are lay-ups. You can't miss. Keep an eye out for these and don't be shy about hopping on the bachelorette party bus or inviting the entire party to move up to your suite at Mandalay Bay for the afterparty. This has been done and it always results in a good time!

## 96. The Switcharoo

Don't even try switching girls after you and your buddy have already kissed them or hooked up. It might be fun trying, but I have never seen it done successfully. It is most likely just a waste of energy.

Party Scars and I tried it one time. We were out late partying. Afterwards we wanted some Taco Bell. In the Taco Bell parking lot there were a couple drunk poptarts scarfing down some Mexican food. I could tell they wanted to party.

We started talking to them. After a little chit chat we told them we knew of an afterparty (all the bars were closed). They said, "Okay, we'll follow you." So we drove to Scars's house. Not the afterparty. We were going in the door when they said, "Hey, this is *your* house." I said, "Wow we must be the first ones here."

After some brief conversation and laughter, Scars tells his girl to come check out his room. I got my girl into his roommate's room. Let the hook up process begin.

My chick and I fooled around, but not all the way. I think Scars got laid but I'm not sure.

Later, I went to the bathroom to go pee. Scars, randomly, was already in there. (It was a shared hallway bathroom) We gave each other the fist. We were snickering and giggling quietly. We were both feeling pretty good, so I said, "Dude, let's try the Switcharoo." Scars said, "Nooo man! It can't be done." Then Scars thought about it. Scars said, "Okay, let's do it." His chick was much hotter than mine so I was up for trying it.

I went to his room. His girl was face down, tired, trying to go to sleep. She was wearing nothing but a white g-string. Her ass was fricken nice. I started rubbing her back and she said, "Ooooh I like that baby." Well that comment gets me all turned on so I slid my boxers off and straddled her, buck naked, and continued with the backrub. She was gyrating her ass all around and acting very sexy. I was sitting on her, giving her this massage, getting really worked up. My schlong was on top of her ass cheeks, grinding up & down as I rubbed the top of her shoulders and then the middle of her back.

This was going much better than I expected.

As I continued this erotic massage, it seemed to me this girl was getting just as worked up as I was. I scooted off for a second, and slid her panties down....and off. Oh yeah....

I got back on top and continued the massage. Now we were both naked, and I could tell this chick was getting wet and she wanted some dick. My hard cock was still rubbing on her ass as I rubbed her shoulders. It was time to slide my cock....

Just then the door opens. Dumbass Party Scars takes a step in and slowly says, "Bill. I need my room."

Oh man, you should have seen the look on this chick's face as she looked at Scars. She thought Scars was the one on top of her with the stiff cock rubbing on her ass. Instead, there is Scars standing in the doorway.

I remember her words were spoken so slowly. "Get. The. Fuck. Off. Me."

I got off. I scurried out of the room. Both chicks were dressed quickly and talking quietly in the living room when I got down there. There was a little tension, but no words were spoken. The girls left soon after. My chick gave me her number on the way out though, which I thought was cool. But I never called that one.

The Switcharoo is impossible and should never be tried.

## 97. Saint V. Day

What is the best night of the year to go out? Very few would guess Saint Valentine's Day. But this is so! The best night to go out looking for chicks is February 14th! Players and gigolos have kept this a secret until now. This is a day like no other. This is the *only* day of the year when you can be 100% sure that every chick out that night is totally single! If they had any dude or boyfriend or any kind of relationship going on, they would be out on a date that night for sure. Furthermore, many chicks want to hook up that night. Either they are feeling a little insecure about not having a Valentine's date, or they just want a man that night because all of their girlfriends have men.

This was clearly evident one St. Valentine's Day in San Diego. Valentine's Day fell on a Friday, so this was truly a great night to go out. I was out with Riki, Erik, and a couple other dudes. We went to some nightclub downtown.

Skip to the chase. There was a hot blond there wearing a black tight skirt and a pink top. I started talking to her. She didn't walk away, but she definitely wasn't giving me signs that I was in. I hung out with her for 30 minutes or so. She was there with another blond, her roommate. They were both solid 8s. Very hot girls.

I went to get a drink at the bar and Erik and Riki were there. Erik said, "Dude that chick is fine!" I said, "Yeah, can you believe she just graduated and now she is a school teacher?" Riki chimed in, "Yeah, but I have seen her before. She was out in Lake Havasu when I was there. She was with about twelve of her girlfriends. She looked so hot in her bikini. She was probably the hottest one there, but she wouldn't hook up with anyone. She wouldn't talk or drink or show her tits or party late night or anything. She's lame dude. You are wasting your time."

Riki's info let me know this girl was a prude. I wasn't surprised. She wasn't giving me a vibe anyway, so it was no big deal. There weren't too many other chicks there to choose from, so I went back over there and hung out with her and a few of her friends on the dance floor. The night got late and people were leaving. We still wanted to party and some guy knew of an afterparty by the beach. I told this chick I was going there and asked if she wanted to go with. She said she would see what her roommate wanted to do. After talking to her roommate they agreed to come, but they needed go back to their place first so her roommate could meet some guy.

Erik, Rummy, and I followed them to their place, also by the beach. We went into their apartment and grabbed beers from the fridge. The roommate disappeared. After ten minutes my girl went to look for her. I went to look for my girl a minute later.

Apparently, my girl walked in on her roommate getting completely pummeled by some guy in her bedroom. I could tell she was surprised to see her roommate having no-holds-barred sex like that. That would make a lasting impression on her.

We all left together and went to go find this party.

When we arrived at the party, only two guys were there, and one of those guys was leaving. What a letdown. The other guy looked and acted like Jeff Spicolli from Fast Times at Ridgemont High. He invited us in. Riki had seen him once or twice before. He was some lounge lizard that you always ran into at afterparties. We decided to stay since there was nothing else to do. We expected more people to show up.

Time goes by and nobody knows where Riki is. He's got to be somewhere in this three bedroom house. After a quick search, we all find Riki in one of the bedrooms watching a porno. Riki, being the good wingman he is, knew that we would end looking for him so he had a porno DVD playing. The five of us sat down and started watching too. I was surprised that this chick was being cool and watching it with us.

We were watching it for a while when Riki elbowed me and nods his head at me to make a move on that chick. I think to myself, fuckit, what do I have to lose? I will make a move; she will deny me, so what. It's late, and I have nothing to lose.

I put my hand on her thigh and rubbed it for a couple minutes. Then, as we are all watching the TV, I start sliding my hand up. I go higher and higher....and now I'm up her skirt....and still going higher. I'm waiting for her to grab my hand and push it away or slap me or something. I keep going and she doesn't stop me. I get all the way to her koochie and I start rubbing that too. She was letting me! I was blown away by this.

My mind did a complete reversal and I was pissed at myself for listening to Riki and not trying something earlier. With all this going through my mind, I smartened up and decided I needed to get this chick into another room.

I grabbed her by the hand and said, "Let's go check out the rest of the house." I get up and she gets up and we walked out and into another room down the hall. I closed the door and started making out with her and grabbing ass. It was on! No sooner than I did this that fricken cockblock Spicolli busts in and says, "No, no, this is my roommate's room, you can't be in here."

What the hell did he care?! He said we had to go into his room, the third room. This fricken guy just wanted to weasel in on my action. Since it was his house I had no choice but to comply. We went into his room.

Immediately, he was trying to give my girl some blow. I passed. She did some, which I found a little surprising. I must have judged this girl all wrong. I had a real sense she was ready to get down and dirty now. While she was leaning over, I reached up her skirt and pulled her panties down and off. She gave minimal resistance. Then I started making out with her. It was on.

Then another damn interruption. Riki wanted in the room too. Riki tried getting in. Spicolli jumped up and pushed on the door to keep him out.

This was a very interesting and hotly contested battle for the door. I remember watching and being very entertained. The door was about two inches open, and both guys were pushing hard.

On the one hand, there was Riki. He lives and dies for gangbangs. He knows how rare they are, and he had the innate sense that one could be in the works. He'll be damned if a gangbang takes place without him! Riki knows if the door is shut and locked, he will never get in.

Riki pushed hard on the door.

On the other hand, there was Spicolli. He too can sense this chick is ready to go. He saw me get her panties off with little resistance. He looks like a dude who rarely gets laid, so this is a big opportunity for him. He thinks if a third guy is in the room, it could ruin the whole situation.

Spicolli pushed back and held the door.

Riki pushed hard. Spicolli held his ground. At first they both acted like they weren't trying that hard, so as to not be embarrassed about fighting over a door. Then Riki pushed harder; then Spicolli pushed back. The cheap door bent and waffled slightly. Spicolli was turning red. It was a real battle!

Riki, the man with the stronger will, finally gave a huge push and backed Spicolli off the door. He walked in out of breath and said, "Hiiiiii," to the girl and then did a line with her. It was funny watching Riki try to act all nice to the girl as he was out of breath.

I leaned back, grabbed my girl, and started making out with her on the bed. All of us were on Spicolli's dumpy queen size bed. I would have preferred to be alone with this chick for sure, but I had to make due. Those guys were caressing her and I was kissing her and trying to get her bra off. I finally did. I looked down and could see Spicolli was down there licking her box already! Geez! You could tell Spicolli hadn't been laid in a long time. He was eating that pussy like it was a last supper.

I got naked. I forced him aside and slipped it in. I was doing her and boy, was it good pussy. Nice and tight and soooo good. I was loving it. I was on top of her, biting her ear while I was pumping her. Then I leaned up so I could see this chick's hot body. Well now Spicolli is directly on my right and Riki is on my left. Three dudes side by side. Both Riki and Spicolli are naked, on their knees beating their meat staring at her.

I was a little flustered by these guys spanking it right next to me, so I tried to just focus on my girl. I started pumping her really hard while I was sitting up holding her thighs. These guys next to me start beating their meat hard and fast. Then I slowed down and pumped her real smooth, and those damn guys slow down too. Then I speeded up and they speeded up too. They were fricken beating off in unison to the same speed as I was fucking. It was really fuckin annoying. I wish I had blinders on like those horses wear in the Kentucky Derby.

I was banging away. She had her face in the pillow and she was loving it. I pulled out and jizzed and got up and walked out.

Veni Vidi Vici!

I walked into the other room and Erik was still in their watching a porno. He was stunned because I was buck naked.

I sat down and he said, "What's going on in there?" I said, "Gangbang."

Erik is not a gangbang guy, and there is nothing wrong with that. I hung out in there and watched the porno and he and I talked about how wrong we were about this chick.

About 10 or 15 minutes later I went back in there. Nothing had changed; these guys were all coked up so they were having major difficulties getting hard-ons. I moved the limp dicks aside and got up on her, straddled her, and put my cock right in her mouth. Riki mumbled, "Good idea Bill." She took my cock like it was a life-support system. It was great head. This chick was cock starved or something. I got really hard again and slid down and started doing her again. She loved it. Man that was good pussy. I pulled out and jizzed on her again. I got my clothes this time and went into the other room.

Those guys had fun with her for another hour and a half. They both finally got hard and took turns boning her. She got banged all night long.

Then the sun started coming up. This girl was a champion but she finally decided she had to go. Riki and Spicolli each did her once and got blowjobs also. We dropped her off at her place and went home.

It was one hell of a great night. Riki and I talked about that story for quite a while. Everybody loved hearing that story. To this day we still believe the only reason that girl got so freaky was because it was Valentine's Day.

I gotta tell the follow up to the story. I didn't see Spicolli for a while. He was a lounge lizard and a beach bum, so I thought I might run into him sooner or later. A couple weeks later I was sitting on the wall at the beach, checking out the waves and the chicks. I saw Spicolli riding by on his skateboard. I said, "Hey!" He didn't recognize me at first. Then he did. He gave me the biggest, "Whaaaaaaat's uuuppp?!" and a bro handshake.

I could tell he was happy to see me and that he had a lot of respect for me for getting him laid. We laughed and talked about that wonderful night for a good twenty minutes. It was great reminiscing about that gangbang. Then he was getting ready to go. In a slightly lower voice like he was telling me a secret, he leaned in close and asked me, "Hey dude, you remember that second time you did her?" I said "Yeah." I knew where this was going. He said, "Where did you blow your load that time?" I said, "Right on top of her box bro." I held my palms out as if to say I'm guilty as charged.

He immediately winced and shook his head like he was about to vomit. I thought he was going to get sick right there.

I thought Spicolli might have gone down on her after I had finished, but I wasn't sure. Now I knew. Poor guy went downtown at the wrong time. I didn't feel much sympathy for him because he did weasel in on that gangbang. I'm sure Spicolli still had one of the best Valentine's Days he's ever had.

## 98. The Hair Show Circuit

I am a connoisseur of women. I think about them. I dream about them. I chase them wherever they go. This has led me off the beaten path to places most men would never dream of venturing. One of these such places are Hair Shows. Hairstylist conventions.

Hair shows are simply chalk full of women. Hot and horny women by the truckloads! Quite frankly, Hair Shows are one of my best kept secrets. I stumbled upon them by chance. Soon thereafter I followed the Hair Show circuit around like a rock star groupie. I knew that by hitting the Hair Show circuit I was delving deep into the realm of scamming on women, becoming a pioneer in my field.

If you like women, you will like Hair Shows. Hair Show Conventions are literally a plethora of hot chicks ready to party. Very few hustlers know about Hair Shows, and I hope it stays that way. Hair shows were my bread and butter for years.

The guy who cut my hair was a Latin gay guy. He must have known I was a player because he said to me, "Beelee, I know jou love da weemin; you should go to da Hair Show wit me. Jou will get sooo many weemen!"

I didn't think much of his recommendation.

I was living in the Bay Area. My buddy Mikey B. was also using the same barber. He told me, "Dude, this guy is right. You need to come to the next Hair Show with me." So I decided I would go. I love road trips. I had nothing to lose. We set plans for the next one in Sacramento.

We drove out to Sacramento and got a cheap room next to the Sacramento Convention Center. I had a buddy that lived out there, Ryan T., and I knew that if the Hair Show was lame, Ryan would hook us up with some good local nightlife spots.

Saturday around 2pm Mikey and I hit the Hair Show. We didn't have a badge or a pass to get in, but it was easy to bullshit our way in. There were hundreds of booths, and a lot of people, and one thing *clearly* stood out. It was all women! Sexy hot women with their hair all done up so they looked good for the convention.

So far, so good.

Mike and I wandered around and what do we find? A bar. Hell yeah! One of those portable little hotel bars they wheeled down to serve drinks to people at the trade show. Nobody there was drinking. So what! Mike and I stopped by and ordered a couple Captain & Cokes. I had a drink in my hand and I was surrounded by women. I was having a good time already.

It was beginning to dawn on me what a wonderful thing I had just stumbled upon. It was all the things I searched for when chasing women, all rolled up into one event.

First and foremost, most of the women at conventions are from out of town, and you know what that means. They want to party.

*Point of Advice: When women are on vacation or away from their hometown, they are at their highest level of horniness.*

Second, these women are hairstylists. Hairstylists are a whole different breed. Hairstylists become hairstylists because they love to party, they were terrible in school, they hate having a boss, and they hate responsibility. Chicks become hairstylists to avoid the corporate world and to avoid a lengthy education. Hairstylists can do their job hungover. They can take time off whenever they want. They can gossip and talk about shopping, hairstyles and cock all day long. By nature, these are party girls! It is in their blood.

Third, these women are surrounded by other women, which means they are man-deprived. Mikey and I are in a convention full of cockstarved lovely women.

We start strolling around. Chicks are checking us out left and right. We were both wearing clothes to party in all night: jeans, a cool dress shirt, and of course, nice pimp shoes. We stood out. Basically, just because we were normal guys we stood out. It was actually a little embarrassing because all these chicks were staring; heads were turning, whispering, etc. There were literally no other guys in the whole place! Well, some gay guys, but they don't count.

We kept strolling around and then some girl grabbed me out of nowhere and said, "I want to give you a manicure." She was older, but still pretty hot. I said Okay. I have never had a manicure before. My guess was she was going to clean my fingernails. She pulled me through this curtain and next thing I know I was on this little stage in front of about 30 chicks. She grabs the microphone and says, "I found a volunteer to show you the best way to perform your manicure using Such&Such product." She proceeded to give me a manicure. It was pretty cool. Mike was cracking up watching me get a manicure in front of all these people.

When I was done I looked around and couldn't find Mikey. I spotted this hot chick giving a presentation on some kind of haircutting technique, and sure enough, there was Mikey in the barber's chair as her guinea pig.

It turns out that there is a complete lack of men at these shows. We were extremely popular, just because we were men! Women knew that if they did their presentation with Mikey or I, two decent looking guys, their audience would be more interested. They were probably so use to having other women or gay guys as their subjects.

Soon after Mike and I learned to say No to most modeling requests. But we did have a couple more cocktails. We began approaching some of the hotter chicks in the booths. Naturally, they always asked what we were doing there. We said we were just doing some modeling, and then I would show them my manicure. Other times we would say Mike's sister was a hairstylist and that we just love the industry. Needless to say, we had no trouble meeting chicks. It was on. Let me repeat. It was on!!!

We talked to a couple hotties and agreed to meet them at a bar later that evening. We had a great time in Sacramento. We both got laid. Me the first night and Mike the second night.

It was a fantastic, fantastic weekend. I could go into detail about the hot chicks we pummeled, but the San Diego Hair Show is a much better yarn.

Mike and I continued to hit the Hair Shows a few times each year. The Hair Show Circuit was and is an absolute goldmine. We went to the one in Las Vegas which was huge; we went to Phoenix, Chicago, San Jose and some others, but the most memorable one was early on in San Diego.

San Diego was only the third or fourth Hair Show we had traveled to, but by then we were seasoned pros. That day I was at the mall picking up some new clothes. I got back to our hotel in Mission Valley in the late afternoon. As soon as I got into the room Mike said, "Dude. I met this *hot* chick and I think she wants to party! Mike's a short little guy, kinda looks like the actor Steve Zahn, well built, big nose, cool blond hair, and a libido like Wilt Chamberlain. He loves women. One of the horniest dudes I have ever met.

Mike went on, "Dude, she has the best rack you have ever seen! She just broke up with her boyfriend!"

I said, "Does she have a friend?"

"Oh dude, she was wearing these tight jeans, and she has big, perfect boobs." He held his hands up like he was squeezing her boobs already. He stared at his hands. He was basically talking to himself.

"Dude, does she have a friend Mikey?"

"Oh man, this chick wants to get boned for sure!"

I repeated, "Mikey, does she have a friend?!"

He finally paid attention and said, "Oh yeah, I think she does have a friend. My chick wants to party!" Mikey rubbed his hands together like the plan was all coming together.

I quizzed him on what her friend looked like. Of course, he was pretty vague about it. He begged me to wingman him on this one though because he really wanted this chick. He said her friend wasn't bad at all. Mike was literally a walking hard-on. That's why I liked him. I agreed to be his wingman.

He went on to tell me how they were at the hotel bar and he got them to do some shots and they were coming over soon. He said they were from Arkansas, here for the Hair Show. Arkansas? Geez, this will be a first.

I quickly analyzed the situation. They were from out of town, which was good. They were doing shots; that was very good. But Mike didn't sound too excited about my chick's looks, that was not good.

Since they were coming over soon, it was still early enough to wingman Mike for a little while and then bail out if my chick was ugly.

The chicks showed up. I was pleasantly surprised with my chick. She was a dirty blond with short curly hair. It looked like it took two hours to make her hair look the way it did. She was about 5'4, innocent-looking, super body, and only 19. I couldn't believe how young she was. Mike's chick was a little hotter; brunette, big tits and 25. They worked together at some salon in Arkansas.

Problem was dumbass Mike had fed them too many shots earlier. You can never give a young girl too many shots because she will get too drunk and you will end up having to babysit her instead of hooking up with her.

We were all hanging out on the king size bed talking, listening to some Steve Miller. Mike was trying to get his chick closer to him so he could go in for a kiss. She was resisting. I figured it was because we were all in the same room. I wanted to separate us somehow.

*Point of Advice: Separating friends is a key element to hooking up.*

I don't remember if I said let's go into the bathroom, or if my chick had to go to the bathroom to get sick. Either way, she and I ended up in the bathroom. She started barfing up tequila.

Most guys would have thrown in the towel right there and given up on this chick. Most guys.

I hung in there. I helped her and consoled her and talked to her and made her brush her teeth. We hung out in the bathroom for what seemed like 30 minutes. She barfed one more time and then she started feeling better. I was standing right behind her at the sink. I was helping her brush her teeth (with Mike's toothbrush) and I was getting pretty close to her. We continued to talk in this position. I would kiss her on the neck every so often. She was wearing this one-piece long tight cloth dress on, really weird outfit. Arkansas fashion I guess. I knew there would be a problem getting that long dress off, if we ever made it that far.

I kept talking to her while standing right behind her. My crotch and my hard-on were pressing into her ass the whole time as we talked. I finally reached down to her ankles and started rubbing her lower leg and kissing her neck. My hand went higher and higher. Her dress was coming up and she wasn't resisting. We haven't even kissed yet but this chick was letting my hand get all the way up to her ass! And boy did she have a nice firm ass. Well now I have a big hard-on. I swiftly used both hands to unbutton my jeans and lower my boxers. My cock popped out like a coiled spring. But the dress dropped back down because I wasn't holding it, so now I gotta do the whole thing over again. I went down to her ankles and slowly rubbed her leg and her inner thigh. The whole time we were talking about something else, don't remember what, and ignoring this sexual foreplay going on.

I remember I started rubbing her box and thought she was going to say stop or something. She did.

She said, "Stop. You don't even have protection."

Little butterflies and white doves started jumping around in my head and I felt like doing an ancient tribal rain dance. I was going to get laid! I was going to get laid!! I contained myself and said calmly, "Yes I do." I pulled a condom out of my back pocket and set it on the sink in front of her. She spun around and started making out with me.

It was a nasty tequila/Colgate barf kiss, but I didn't care.

Now that I am writing this I remember how nasty that kiss was. Fuckin gross. Anyway, I was really horned up. I slid her purple Sears Roebuck panties off, and then took off my shirt and shoes. My jeans were at my ankles so I went for her dress. If she let me take this long cloth thing off, she would be completely naked. I know from experience, many chicks are very uncomfortable being naked. Furthermore, the lights were on bright. However, this chick was only 19 so she was fearless, and she had a bunch of tequila in her. So I went for the dress.

The dress came off without a hitch. Whew!

I grabbed the condom and put it on.

I worked it in. We boned standing up for a while. I was squeezing her tight body. She was holding me tightly. It was great. Suddenly she said to me, "Lay down." I was like, 'Wow this chick is calling the shots?' I laid down flat on the bathroom floor. Toes touching the door, head touching the bathtub. She came over me and sat down on me and started riding my cock! She still had her feet on the ground, just going up & down on my cock. It was fricken awesome.

Everything was going good when all of a sudden she jumped up and muttered, "I want to try something." I wasn't paying attention to what she said; I just wanted to keep fucking this hot little sex kitten. We got up. I bent her over so she had her left hand on the bathtub. With her other hand she was trying to get my cock back in her. I was looking in the mirror at her nice boobs flopping around. I was thinking, 'Man this is so, so awesome!' After a while I was wondering what's taking her so long to put me back in. I wasn't really paying attention, but I look down and she is trying to stuff my big hog into her tiny ass. And it's already half way in! I remember thinking, "Holyyyyyy shit!"

She continued to try and work it in. It was an amazing thing watching her try to stuff my big cock in her tight little ass. I was so turned on!!!!! After a few minutes she gave up and said, "Ugghh I can't." She pulled it out and put it back in her pussy. I start railroading her really hard as she was bent over, holding onto the bathtub. I was watching everything in the mirror too; it was pretty damn erotic. Fuckin really good sex.

Of course her friggin bimbo friend outside starts knocking on the door. I thought the party might be over so I started really giving it to my chick hard and fast. I blew my load and boy was it fuckin great.

I pulled out. She went to the door and said, "Just a few more minutes," like nothing was going on.

Then, this princess turns to me, sits on the toilet and says, "Don't worry, I'll get you off."

She thought I hadn't finished yet and she was going to suck it until I did! What a good girl! I was all for it. She peeled the rubber off and could see the big mess that came with it. She realized I already blew my load. We cleaned up quickly while her damn friend kept knocking on the door saying, "Are you Okay?" We finally walked out. My chick wanted to go home. So did the other one. Standard. They wasted no time and gave their phone numbers to us and left.

I was on cloud nine. I sat on the edge of the bed and then fell back on the bed in utter happiness.

Mikey was just the opposite. Apparently, they had made out and that's it. He had spent the better part of an hour trying to get her blouse off to play with her titties. He got denied the entire time. He was pretty frustrated when he told me this. He finally said, "Did you get anywhere with that other chick?" I said, "Yeah, I put it in her ass, but it was too big for her, so we just fucked in the tub." He wasn't amused. And he sure as hell didn't believe me. He mumbled, "Yeah right," as he turned on the TV. I knew he wouldn't believe me.

I turned the TV off, turned towards him, looked him in the eye and said, "Mike, I know you won't believe this, but I swear this is the truth...." and then I proceeded to tell the entire story, leaving out no details.

It was very anti-climactic though. Even though I was looking him in the eye and telling him the truth, I still think he doubted me. He was bitter. It was, however, the best time I ever had at a Hair Show.

## 99. Fishbowl Parties

Many hot streaks take place in the summertime. A guy and his crew can go their entire summer on a hot streak. One of the results of a nice hot summer is a large amount of random chick's phone numbers. The best way to handle an over abundance of phone numbers is a Fishbowl Party.

Many summers ago I was broke as a joke. I had just moved to San Diego and was sleeping on my friend's, Tommy and Jeff's, couch. It was the beginning of summer and we were going out all the time and I mean *all* the time. Jeff and Tommy were dialed in all over the town. We weren't paying covers. They knew everyone in La Jolla, Pacific Beach, and downtown SD. They had a great townhouse pad right near the beach in La Jolla.

Before we went out, I would pound a 40 oz of Mickey's Malt Liquor to get a buzz going. Then once there, I would lurk near the dance floor and snake people's drinks as they set their drinks down to dance. If I met a chick and she wanted a drink, I'd tell her I'll be right back. I'd come back with two unknown cocktails and tell her the damn bartender must have screwed up.

*Point of Advice: When low on the cash flow, hang out near the dance floor. There's an abundance of full cocktails on the outskirts of the dance floor waiting to be borrowed.*

I was broke, but I was surviving.

We were meeting chicks by the dozens that summer. I had no apartment, no money for dates, no car, and no job. But I was getting laid all the time. That couch in the living room was being put to good use.

We had a great network of friends. Some lived downtown, some were up in LA and they would visit often, and some were down by the beach. This was the late 90s and few rolled out with cell phones yet. Soon Tommy's kitchen counter was full of napkins with phone numbers on them, matchbooks with phone numbers on them, business cards, etc. Just phone numbers everywhere.

To clean up the place we put all the phone numbers in this big empty fishbowl on the shelf near the living room. We didn't necessarily want to call these phone numbers - we were too busy working new chicks, but we knew there was some value in all those numbers. Half way through the summer we came up with the idea of having a big party. It would be at the end of summer, right after Labor Day. We would call *all* of the numbers in the fishbowl, and invite them to a huge, end of summer party. We said that the only rule is that if the chick's number is in the fishbowl, she has to be called no matter what.

It was a great idea. It inspired us to go out and be even more aggressive with chicks. If a girl didn't want to come home with us and party that night, we just got her number and threw it in the fishbowl. One night I made out with three different chicks, scored with the last one, and added three numbers to the fishbowl in the morning. It was a satisfying feeling adding numbers to the fishbowl. Our entire crew was getting in on it too. Some buddies said, "Dude, I needed a place to put all these damn numbers. What a great idea!" Some of our buddies had steady girlfriends. They were happy to finally have a place to put the phone numbers they acquired while out with us. Normally, they would just throw them away.

This was a big fishbowl, and it was overflowing with pieces of paper, napkins, bathroom tissue with numbers in lipstick, matchbooks, and business cards. It was quite a collection. Near the end of summer we planned out the fishbowl party. We decided to have it at Todd's house. He had a big house. His roommates were slobs and the place was never clean. Perfect for a party. One night Tommy, Jeff, Mexicuddler, Pat, and I bought a case of beer, put on some Bob Marley, and emptied out the fishbowl. We began calling all the numbers. That in itself was pretty damn fun. Mexicuddler (Kevin) was our buddy from PB. He earned that nickname because he was slightly chubby, 25% Mexican, and he was infamous for cuddling with chicks instead of trying to hook up with them. He hated his nickname, but it stuck.

Mexicuddler had to call this chubby chick he got a handjob from earlier that summer. He told us about getting her number. She made him swear up and down that he would call her the next day. He said, "I promise I will call you. I promise!" He didn't. Now it was a month later and he was dreading this phone call. We told him, "Dude, that's the rule. You have to call." He was lucky. It went straight to voicemail. He just left the address and date of the party.

I remember my buddy Pat calling this chick he met in the middle of summer. I was there when he met her. She was not very good looking. Her face looked like a piece of worn leather because she obviously hadn't used sunscreen for the past seventy years. Pat put in overtime punching the clock with this broad when he met her; he was really horny that day and she had a decent body. By the end of the day Leather Face was completely into him, but wouldn't go home with him. Now he was calling her and we could all hear her say, "You met me two months ago and now you call me for the first time?! Just to invite me to some stupid party?! What the hell is that?! I can't believe you!!" She was really ranting and raving and he had to hold the phone a few inches away from his ear. Pat was caught off guard and could only respond with, "It's going to be a pretty fun party." We were all crackin up at him getting chewed out.

I had to call four chicks that I had pummeled. Those were uncomfortable phone calls. I was hoping to get voicemail and, of course, every one of them answered. I couldn't get off the phone quick enough. The other guys could hear my awkward conversation and they were cracking up.

A majority of the phone numbers in the fishbowl were unfamiliar to all of us. We called the chicks and tried to explain that someone here got their phone number and we just wanted to invite them to a party.

Some chicks said sure. Some chicks said, "Don't ever call me again." Some wanted to figure out what, where, and how we got their phone number. A few wanted to talk and have a conversation and we couldn't get them off the phone.

We gave the address of the party to every girl we talked to and every voicemail that answered. It took a couple hours and a case of beer, but we made it through the whole fishbowl. We crumpled up all those phone numbers and finally threw them in the trash.

The day of the party came and it was a huge success. We had three kegs and a full bar. Todd had set up speakers on his roof deck and we were cranking Jay Z's *'Girls, girls, girls'* as people began showing up. It was sweet. A couple hundred people showed up to the party and the place was really rockin. We were amazed at how many chicks actually showed up. We had a ratio of probably two girls to every guy, at least. That is terrific for a house party.

It was hilarious trying to figure out who some of these chicks were. Some of them looked familiar but we couldn't remember from where. The chick Mexicuddler called showed up just to chew him out, and then she left. I hooked up with this chick that I had left a voicemail for telling her about the party. I had gotten her number a month ago but the bitch never returned my phone call. She dogged me, and now she shows up to the party and she was all over me - quite surprising. I was fine with that though. I was working on getting her drunk. Riki and Mexicuddler had this hot Russian girl cornered by the bar and they were both trying to put the moves on her. Brady brought his girlfriend and she was doing shots of tequila because they were fighting and arguing because Brady kept looking at other chicks. Pat was hooking up with Leather Face; yeah, she showed up. Some chick Party Scars knew showed up. She dumped a drink on his head, then stayed and partied. Really early on Todd boned some Brazilian chick outside in the bushes. She had the nicest ass I have ever seen and an absolute trainwreck for a face. Butter, bigtime. But it was cool that Todd scored so early. It set the tone for the party and made the rest of us want to get laid even more.

The party was really crackin. We had a disco ball, black light, and hip-hop going off in the living room. I walked by and the entire room was dancing and singing to 'Baby I got your money' by ODB. It was off the hook! Tommy and Jeff both hooked up with hot blond sisters on the dance floor. Later on it was time close so I took my chick into Todd's bedroom and accidentally walked in on Riki getting a hummer from the drunk Russian chick. We went into another bedroom. Carter was in there hooking up with some cougar so we had to look elsewhere. I opened the door to the third bedroom and Brady was in there deadhorsing his girlfriend. I finally found an empty room and after a little coercion, I got a nice little hummer from my chick. I told her to just go down on me for a minute. Then when a minute was up I said, "Oh don't stop baby, just don't stop," like it was the best hummer of all time, even though it wasn't. You gotta sell it sometimes.

I saw Riki in the bathroom afterwards and he said he banged out the hot Russian girl just a minute ago. He and I touched fists and I said, "Right on bro."

I remember thinking this party was a great fricken idea. I saw Derek hooking up with one of my retreads and he was looking for an empty room. I looked in Todd's room to help him out. Mexicuddler was in there lying on the bed making out with the drunk Russian girl. Ooofah!

He turned and saw us and gave us a smile and a thumbs up.

We left and closed the door and Derek found a different room. Two chicks got into a fight on the dance floor and that was fun to watch but it messed up the tone of the party. Things began to die down after that. It turned out to be just a great party though.

We had another Fishbowl Party the following summer. It was just as good. Keep those random phone numbers. There's value in those numbers.

## 100. Spring Break

I love college girls. Chicks do not look any hotter than they do in college. College girls are the top of the food chain. College girls make the world go around.

You know what else I love? I love girls on vacation. Girls on vacation are so much fun. Girls on vacation lose all their inhibitions. They go wild. They get drunk. They get naked. They get slutty. They want to hook up to make the vacation memorable. They want to hook up because all their friends will be hooking up and they don't want to look like a loser. They do things they would never dream of doing back at home.

Only one time of the year are you guaranteed to find the combination of these two. *Spring Break!* College girls on vacation!! It doesn't get any better baby! More crazy stories and wild hook-ups occur during Spring Break than any time of the year.

Spring Break needs to be a destination for every single man. Riki and I and friends go every year. Every Spring Break we've been on was a fricken blast. Lake Havasu, Cancun, Daytona Beach, Miami, Las Vegas, South Padre Island, Cabo San Lucas, San Felipe, Rosarito, the Bahamas, you name it.

Spring Break was fun in college, but after college, we really stepped up our Spring Break game. Riki is the Mel Kiper of Spring Breaks. He knows everything. In January he will start emailing us out possible destinations for that year. He will find every college's Spring Break schedule, so we know which school is off that week. This is important. Spring Break isn't one week, it's four. East Coast Spring Break stars in early March. West Coast Spring Break starts in April. Four weeks of debauchery. Riki knows which schools are the party schools. He knows the Spring Break promoters and where the big trips are. In college, Spring Break lasted one week. After college, Spring Break was a month-long vacation.

We all had more money than we did in college, so we would go all out on Spring Break. We'd get the Presidential Suite whenever possible. The best room in the hotel. Chicks would see our room and their panties would get wet. They'd call their girlfriends to come see it and hang out. We'd stock the room with top shelf alcohol. We'd have bottles of Jagermeister, Patron, Kettle One, champagne, Red Bull, and all mixers. Somebody would bring a deluxe blender for margaritas. Mimosas in the morning. Margaritas all day by the pool. Shots of Patron during pregame.

College chicks are always broke. They'd love coming to are room to get some free, top shelf alcohol. Much better than the jungle-juice they were use to. Getting drinks in our room would make them comfortable hanging out at our place, a key ingredient for hooking up later. We'd also bring a giant boom box, one that attaches to and plays ipods. We had thumpin' hip hop playing all night, reggae music playing all day.

In Cancun we all chipped in for a bodyguard. A bodyguard? Yeah, a bodyguard. One of our buddies knew this huge 400 lb black guy. We paid for his flight, got him a dumpy hotel room, and gave him $500 bucks cash. He was our bodyguard every night. We didn't need a bodyguard at all. Who were we?! But you should see the attention we'd get at the nightclubs. Chicks would see a huge black guy in a black suit and sunglasses guarding our table. They would want to know what the hell was going on. He would be a dick to chicks unless they were hot. We got so much ass just because of that bodyguard.

In South Padre Island we all brought elaborate 70s costumes. Not the cheap ones; full on 70s outfits that we had fitted perfectly by a tailor. We had long, knee-length jackets, styling hats, polyester pants, boas, the whole nine yards. We also brought unique goblets to carry around for our drinks, just like Snoop Dog. The first night we went out, we owned it! We were on fire. Even better, the whole rest of the trip, where ever we went, people recognized us. It was so easy to hook up.

Man, Spring Break is the best. Spring Break every year. Don't miss it!

## 101. Benefits Of Travelling

My favorite thing to do is to travel. Flying or driving, it doesn't matter. There are many, many wonderful benefits that come from traveling. All of these benefits will, in one way or another, lead to you becoming more successful with women.

The first and most obvious benefit of traveling are the great times you will have on that vacation or weekend getaway. The memories and stories and laughs that I have from vacations are priceless; I wouldn't trade them for anything in the world. The places you see, the people you meet, and the women you hook up with provide every reason to jump on a plane and *go somewhere.*

A majority of your trips will be made to destinations where other people are also on vacation. What does this means? Chicks on vacation! And when chicks are on vacation, they want to party. Girls get in a completely different mood when they are on vacation; they lose their inhibitions, they are care-free, and they want to do things they normally don't do. Be prepared to meet fun girls on vacation.

You can really concentrate on partying and meeting chicks while on vacation, much more so than when you are home. You have all day to lie on the beach and plan out your night of partying. You can meet chicks during the day, tell them you are on vacation, and ask them out for dinner that night. Or you can ask them what they recommend for nightlife. Then meet up with them later. Chicks know you are from out of town. They will let their guard down and want to party with you because they know there are no strings attached.

Another benefit of traveling is your travel buddies. You might go on a trip with one good buddy, and a couple friends of friends. By the end of the trip, you'll all be life-long pals. I still keep in touch with just about everybody I have ever been on a trip with. A road-trip is a bonding experience, and that's cool. When I see or run into guys I have traveled with, we always have some good laughs remembering things that happened on that trip. Some of my best friends to this day are six guys I went down to Tijuana with for a one-night road trip. We barely knew each other. We decided to have a dog fight down there. It was one hilarious little road trip. Since then, I've been on dozens of other trips with those guys.

When you are on vacation, you can always have the attitude of, "I am never going to see these people again." This is why your game is naturally better on vacation. Chicks read your I-don't-give-a-shit attitude and that is a turn-on.

The knowledge benefit is significant as well. Once you have been to whichever destination you decide on, you will acquire knowledge of that place. This can be invaluable! Every time you meet a chick who has also been to that place you two will have something in common. Some of the best conversations start when two people have visited the same place. I have now been to so many cities in America, and so many international countries, I can talk to a chick about almost any place she has been to.

This also makes it easier for you to date foreign women once you are back in America. You will have better understanding of foreign culture. You can relate to them. You can understand where they are coming from.

One good time happened in Barcelona, Spain. Barcelona is a fabulous city. Riki and Tommy and I were there on a short two night stay. We were on our way to Pamplona for Running Of The Bulls. That night we hit up some local nightclub/bar near the harbor in Barcelona.

The chicks were definitely checking us out. We obviously stood out as foreigners or tourists. We were getting drunk, listening to the DJ spin some Shapeshifters. It was still early.

There were some young Australian girls there partying and from my travel experiences I know two things about Australians: they love to travel and they love to party. These chicks were on some budget European bus tour with a short stopover in Barcelona. The cute blond of the bunch had a smokin hot body. I turned on the charm. After a little conversation and a lot of flirting, I pulled her out of there. Her friends were being cockblocks, so I had to sneak her out the back door before they pulled her away from me.

She & I made the long walk through Los Robles back to my hotel, avoiding all the damn pick-pockets in that city.

Got her back up into my hotel room. We were kissing and getting naked.

I couldn't believe my luck. This blond was ridiculously hot. Like a young Nicole Kidman. I was removing her clothing and counting my blessings. She was so submissive and wanting to please. I'll never forget her caressing my schlong ever so gently as I slid off her skirt. Her head was tilted to the side and she was looking at my schlong and caressing it like it was the golden god of pleasure. She dropped to her knees and started giving me head.

I gradually guided her up and onto the bed. Bent her over and, ever so slowly, slid my cock in....it was so erotic I almost blew my load right there. I kept going...slowly. I reached my hands around and grabbed her perfect tits. I grabbed them firmly...and then I started giving it to her....firm....then hard....then harder. It was some amazing sex man. I flipped her over and did her missionary. I eventually pulled out and jizzed on her stomach.

I fell over onto the bed, happy as could be.

She got up and went to the bathroom.

I was wondering what she was doing. She ran the sink until the hot water warmed up. She dampened a cloth with warm water and came back. She used the warm cloth to clean me up. Wow! She gently cleaned my crotch and my penis. The warm cloth was so soothing. She was so gentle and caring. Then she dried me off with a towel. She went back to the bathroom and came back. She curled up next to me in the fetal position. She put her left hand under my shoulder and rested her hand right on my soft penis. She began to fall asleep. I had both my hands under my head. What a nice and caring girl!

Man, that chick was such a good girl; I still think about her to this day. What blew me away about this chick was the ride home.

She woke me up an hour later. It was only 1am but she told me how her bus tour was leaving early in the morning and she couldn't miss it. She had to leave. This being a foreign city and a little dangerous, I was worried about her going alone. I decided to accompany her in a taxi ride back to her place.

Her place was all the way across town. We flagged down a taxicab and hopped in. She was snuggling up next to me. She was so hot - I was going to miss her. I was pretty exhausted from that sexual encounter, but still a little horny because she was so attractive and so submissive. I put her hand on my crotch. She started rubbing it. I got worked up again, so I took my johnson out and kind of gave her a nudge to go down there. She did! She went down on me in the taxi. She sucked on my cack for the *entire* ride back to her place. A good twenty minutes. I was amazed! So was the cab driver. This chick knew she would never see me again and yet she continued to go down on me for the entire cab ride home.

I couldn't bust a damn nut though. We arrived at her place. It was pretty much a campground and they were all staying in tents. I had to get out of the taxi and walk her through these gates and through the campground. I gave her a long kiss goodbye. I was on the verge of telling her to abandon her bus tour and stay with me a few days. But I had to let that sweet child fly away.

I walked back and my taxi was gone. Fuck. I was a long way from my hotel. It was 2 am and the streets were deserted. I walked a mile looking for a taxi.

The coast wasn't far away and I could hear some music. I walked up on a local nightclub. They were playing some jazzy house music, sounded pretty good. There were no taxis outside. The place looked interesting. It was 2 am, fuck it, let's check it out.

It was all Spanish locals. It was late, but the place was going *off*. Packed with people. Everyone was dancing. I was in a pretty good mood myself, so I made my way to the bar and ordered a San Miguel. I had no idea where I was, but I had a cold beer in my hand, I had just got laid, and I was in a bar that was going off. *This* is why I love travelling.

And it was about to get better.

I was totally happy just drinking a beer by the bar. It hadn't even crossed my mind yet how I was going to get home. Two Spanish senoritas slid up next me and ordered some drinks at the bar. One of them was cute. The other was drop dead gorgeous cute.

They were both wearing slinky fly away skirts, the kind only beautiful Spanish chicks can wear. They were both in their mid 20s. I waited a few minutes before I said anything.

If I would have hit on them immediately, I would have looked like just another horny tourist. If I waited, they would be thinking, "Why is this guy not hitting on us?" I already assumed that it was no mistake that they were ordering drinks right next to me. I must have stood out in the bar. Finally, I said to the hottest one, "You really have beautiful hair. I'm sure you get that compliment all the time."

Before she could respond I heard a voice behind me. It was a deep voice. "Don't talk to my fucking girlfriend motherfucker." Uh-oh. Immediately, I felt something pointy like a finger in the middle of my back. Uh-oh!

I should have been worried. But the voice had no accent. It was American. And it sounded familiar! I spun around and Riki gave me a big "What's up bro?!!"

We were both wondering what the other guy was doing in this random nightclub on the outskirts of Barcelona. Riki was with the two girls. He met the cute one at the bar we were originally at earlier that night. They both hit it off. She brought him to this place to show him more of Barcelona. He lost Tommy and me at the first bar. Her gorgeous friend met them here, and she was single.

Jackpot!!!

I explained to Riki how I happened upon this place and we had a good ole laugh. He introduced me to both chicks. The gorgeous one was a lay-up. We hit off right away and were making out within minutes. She was a waitress and an aspiring model. She was full of life and we talked for a long time. She was very genuine and talked with a lot of passion. She had the body of a goddess and beautiful, voluptuous lips. Wooo, she was hot man. I was smitten.

We stayed and danced and drank. I bought a cigar and smoked it at our table. The jazz music mix was fantastic. Riki and I kept laughing at the coincidence of running into each other.

Both girls lived together, not far away. We went back to their place. It was not a nice place. But so what. Riki and I split up and went into different bedrooms. I pounded out my bronze Spanish goddess two times. She was incredible. She was so nice and sweet and yet she was a wildchild in bed. She did some crazy things and we laughed and had sex for hours. It was euphoria. She wanted to marry me, and I wanted to marry her. But the sun was coming up and I had flight to catch.

I will never forget walking out of there. I walked out onto the street of a country I had never been to before. Across the street was the Mediterranean Sea. The sun was rising and glistening off the water and shining right on me. I had jeans on and an unbuttoned white dress shirt blowing in the breeze. My hair was all messed up and sticking straight up. My hands and whole body smelled like cigars and sex. Somebody off in the distance was playing some Spanish jazz music as they woke up. I realized I loved that music. Riki came walking out a minute after I did. He came up to me; no words we spoken, just happy smirks. Our hands made a clapping sound as we gave each other a bro handshake and turned and began to walk. I think he felt the same way I did. At that point I realized that this was one of the greatest feelings a guy could ever have. Wow, what a night. As the sun beat down on us we told each other about our experiences. We walked along the coast looking for a cab as the sun came up. That feeling and that sunrise will always be embedded in my mind. It's a feeling I'll forever be chasing.

# GLOSSARY

A-GAME - The best game you have to score with women.

ARMY CRAWL - Crawling down low to get into a bedroom to witness or partake in a hook up.

BANG - *verb*. To have sex, to bone, to pummel.

BUTTER - Girl with a hot body and very ugly face. Derived from: Everything is good *but her* face.

CAR WASH - A sexual move; covering your cock with heaps of whip cream and then lowering it above girl's face and swaying back and forth, giving her a car wash.

CIRCUS BOOBS - A bad boob job. Fake boobs that look out of proportion on a chick's body.

COMMANDO - Not wearing underwear.

COCKBLOCK - Guy who prevents other guys from getting laid. The lowest male species

COTTAGE CHEESE ASS - A girl's big ass that has ugly dimples like a mound of cottage cheese.

COUGAR - An overly aggressive single woman, 30-45, dressing and acting like she is in her early 20s.

DEADHORSING - Making love to your girlfriend while she is passed out in your bed.

DEER IN THE HEADLIGHTS - A female who is not accustomed to being hit on, or not use to being in the bar/club scene.

DIGITS - Phone number.

DIME PIECE - A hot chick, a 10.

DIRTY SANCHEZ - Doing a girl from behind, putting your index finger in her bunghole, then reaching around and wiping the same finger on her upper lip. It will smell badly every time she breathes through her nose, thus, dirty. She will also have a light brown mustache - thus, sanchez. Hence: Dirty Sanchez.

DOG FIGHT - Bunch of guys throwing in money, betting on who will hook up with the ugliest chick by the end of the night. Ugliest hook-up wins the money.
Rules for a Dog Fight: 1) Minimum standards for hooking up = making out with tongue. 2) Every guy must throw in the minimum entry (usually $20 to $50), even if he doesn't plan on hooking up with an ugly chick. 3) No bribing ugly chicks to makeout with you. 4) Dogfights are not allowed on your home turf (You don't want people to recognize you participating in a dogfight.) 5) Hooking up with multiple ugly chicks to increase your chances of winning....is permitted. 6) No one-man Dog Fights. 7) Telling hot chicks you are currently in a Dog Fight is *not* permitted. 8) Hooking up with hot chicks while in a Dog Fight is permitted, but you forfeit your $20 bucks. 9) All participants get one vote for the Dog Fight winner; ties are decided by nearest bartender. 10) No dating girls from a Dog Fight once the Dog Fight is over.

DRUNK-DIALING - Calling somebody late night when you are intoxicated and regretting it the next day.

FISHBOWL PARTY - Party where you call and invite all the random phone numbers you have collected over a summer.

FOO FOO DRINK - A daiquiri, pina colada, a drink with an umbrella in it, or any feminine drink.

FRIEND-TO-FRIEND - When you have to have a talk with a friend and set him straight.

FUMBLE - *verb.* Occurs when a chick wants to party and she's all ready to go but you blow it somehow.

FUGLY - *abbr.* Fucking ugly.

GANGBANG - Multiple sexual partners.

GILF - A milf who's kids have kids.

GOLDDIGGER - Chick who wants a guy for his money.

GREASE - *verb.* To pay off, to juice, to bribe.

GRENADE - An ugly chick hanging out with an attractive chick.

GREYSTOKE - A grey-haired guy at the bar who dresses like an old guy but tries to act like a young buck. Greystokes hunt 21-29 year-old money grubbing party girls. As with 'cougar,' a greystoke is not defined solely by age. They are defined by their dress. Greystokes often wear blazers, Gold Oyster Rolex's, loafers with tassels, and Tommy Bahama gear on the weekends.

GROUPER - a 'G.' One thousand.

HAT TRICK - Scoring three times.

HORNY EIGHT'S PHENOMENON - A seldom seen phenomenon that occurs when there is an overabundance of women at a venue, and an unusually abnormal amount of these women are gorgeous. These super hot 9s and 10s make the 7s and 8s uncomfortable. All of the 7s and 8s become insecure and attention-starved. This leads to normally proud and hard-to-score-with 8s becoming very horny & slutty and easy to score with.

JUNGLE BEAVER - Private parts on a female that are not shaved. Au naturaal, winter bush, etc.

HUMMER - Blowjob, bj, going down, head.

HUMP & DUMP - A short term relationship. Also known as: A one-timer. Wine em, dine em, 69 em. Hit it & quit it. Tagged it & red flagged it.

L-BOMB - Love, I love you.

LANDING STRIP - Neatly shaved, long strip of pubic hairs on a female.

LEATHER FACE - Cougar who's face looks like worn leather because she's been in the sun too long.

LEVEL 3 CLINGON - Girl who smothers you, demands all your attention, time, and freedom.

LEVEL 5 CLINGON - Girl who stalks you, calls you 24/7, refuses to break up with you, etc.

LIGHTWEIGHT - Person who can't handle their liquor.

LINEBACKER - A thick chick.

LUSH - Person who drinks too much; a drunkard.

MAN-UP - To be a man, to be brave in a situation. To sack up, to have some balls, to have some guts, to step up.

MEXICAN WILD DOG BOOBS - Older chick with nasty, saggy boobs - similar to those saggy boobs you see on a wild dog that just had babies roaming the streets in Mexico.

MILE HIGH CLUB - To be a member you must have had sex on an airplane during a flight.

MILF - A mom you want to have sex with.

NAKED ELEVATOR - Game where each person in an elevator removes their clothing, in turn, one item at a time. One person removes an article of clothing, then it is the next person's turn. When everyone has removed the first article of clothing, player 1 removes his/her second article of clothing as quickly as possible, and so on. Players continue to quickly remove clothing until a) everyone is naked b) someone refuses and they are the loser, or c) the doors open. A loser of Naked Elevator should feel completely ashamed.

NAKED NINJA - Unauthorized cockblocking maneuver where a friend, stark naked, *suddenly* enters into a room where you are hooking up with a chick, shocking the girl and trying to make you laugh. Blurting out "Naked ninja!!" is optional.

NBC - Natural Born Cockblock

NEW BOOBS PHASE 1 - A two month phase occurring immediately after receiving a new boob job. During this phase the female goes hogwild slutty because she can now attract higher level males who previously were not interested.

PANTY-DROPPER - Super phat house, condominium, hotel suite, view, or jacuzzi. When a girl sees it, she will become so excited she will literally drop her panties and want to have sex immediately.

PANTY GAME - Game played with girls at a bar. You use all your intuition to judge the exact color, fabric, and style of a girl's panties. Her fashion sense, her personality, the mood she is in, and how horny she appears to be *all* must be taken into account. Based on this, you try to guess what kind of panties she has on. Afterwards, the girl has to guess what kind of underwear you have on.

PHONE NUMBER GUY - A guy who's only goal or expectation is to get a girl's phone number. A non-closer.

PISSING GANGSTER STYLE - Peeing with your pants dropped all the way to your ankles.

POPTART - 18 to 23 year-old hot chick in the mood to party.

PUMMEL - *verb*. To have sex, to bone, to bang.

RBV - Red bull & vodka.

RETREAD - Chick that one of your buddies has previously hooked up with.

RODEO SCREW - During sex with a girl, calling her by a different girl's name multiple times, on purpose, then trying to hold on for 8 seconds while she tries to get away.

ROTATION - Group of girls that you are dating.

SCAMMING - *verb*. Picking up on a girl, hitting on a chick, working wool, punching the clock, etc.

SAUSAGE FEST - A party with way too many guys. A sword fight, a dude ranch, a locker room, a cockfight.

SLUMPBUSTER - An ugly chick that you hook up with to break an unsuccessful streak.

SNUGGLE LOCKDOWN - When your sappy buddy cannot, or will not, go out with his buddies because he chooses to stay in with his girlfriend and cuddle and snuggle. Example: "Uh, where is Erik tonight?" "He's not coming out; he's in snuggle lockdown."

S.O.L. - Shit outa luck.

STROBE LIGHT HONEY - A chick that looks great on the dancefloor and in the club, then the lights come on and her true uglyness is revealed.

SUGAR MOMMA - Chick who has more money than the guy she is dating.

TAINT - Area of skin below your testicals and above your bung-hole. 'It taint your ass and it taint your balls.'

TEA BAG - Testicals in the mouth.

THE SHOCKER - Two in the pink, one in the stink.

TRAMPSTAMP - Tattoo above a chick's ass.

TUG JOB - A hand job, a reacharound, a handy.

TWO-PUMP-CHUMP - Guy who gives a very poor performance in bed.

WALK OF SHAME - A girl walking home in the morning wearing the same clothes she went out in the night before. She keeps her head down and walks faster than normal to hasten the embarrassing situation.

WAR STORIES - Stories from previous weekends about encounters with girls while out in the field of battle.

WINGMAN - Buddy who is with you trying to meet girls.

WIFEBEATER - White ribbed sleeveless under-shirt.

WORLD CUP - Bar game where two people in the bar exchange shirts permanently just like soccer players do after a soccer game.

WOUNDED GAZELLE - A very intoxicated drunk girl, stumbling around, ready to be hooked up with. Term derived from the Serengeti in Africa where lions search out the wounded gazelle because they are the easiest prey.

Made in the USA
Las Vegas, NV
07 August 2021

27713790R00138